THE NEW COOKBOOK FOR POOR POETS
(and Others)

REVISED & ENLARGED

The NEW COOKBOOK for POOR POETS (and others)

REVISED & ENLARGED

by Ann Rogers

CHARLES SCRIBNER'S SONS / NEW YORK

For PEGGY, MON AMIE

Copyright © 1979, 1966 Ann Rogers

Library of Congress Cataloging in Publication Data

Rogers, Ann.
   The new cookbook for poor poets (and others).

   Includes index.
   1. Cookery. I. Title.
TX715.R725   1979   641.5   78–23753
ISBN 0–684–16046–3

This book published simultaneously in the
United States of America and in Canada—
Copyright under the Berne Convention

All rights reserved. No part of this book
may be reproduced in any form without the
permission of Charles Scribner's Sons

1 3 5 7 9 11 13 15 17 19   V/C   20 18 16 14 12 10 8 6 4 2

Printed in the United States of America

CONTENTS

FOREWORD   vii
PREFACE TO THE REVISED EDITION   viii
INTRODUCTION   1
    The Nickel Dinner and How It Grew   8
SOUPS   13
    Hot Soups for Cold Days   14
    Cold Soups for Hot Days   18
SALADS   23
    Not-Quite Salads   23
    Hungry Poet Salads   26
    Four Necessary Dressings   31
BUILDING WITH EGGS AND CHEESE   33
    Ways with Eggs   33
    Omelets   37
    Dishes Incorporating Both Eggs and Cheese   39
BEANS, PEAS, RICE, AND ASSORTED CEREALS   46
    Bean Dishes from Canned Beans   47
    Bean Dishes from Dried Beans   51
    Peas   53
    Rice   56
    Pasta   63
ONE POTS   69
    One Pots that Require No Meat   69
    One Pots with Meat   75
MEATS   86
    Beef   87
    Lamb   93
    Pork   96
    Veal   98
    Ground Beef   102
    Variety Meats   106
    Chicken   112

BREADS 124
- Glorifying Store Bread 125
- Two Unusual Breads 128
- Scones and Quick Breads 129
- Crackers 134
- A Yeast Bread for Busy Poets 136
- Breadloaves 136

DESSERTS 142
- Fruits—In Season and Out 142
- Cookies 148
- Desserts from Another Time and Place 156

GILDING THE LILY 163
- Relishes from Jars and Tins 164
- Vinegars 169
- Seasoning Salts 171
- Jellies 171
- Yogurt 172

POOR POET TRIFLES 173

THE NICKEL DINNER AND HOW IT'S CHANGED 175

SOUPS 177
- More Hot Soups for Cold Days 177
- More Cold Soups for Hot Days 181
- A Jar of Bouillon Cubes 181

SALADS 184

SUM AND SUBSTANCE 189
- Eggs and Cheese 189
- Peas, Beans, Rice, and Grains 192
- Pasta 196
- Fish 198
- Miscellanea 200
- Three Snacks for the Poor Poet's Work Space 203

DESSERTS 205
- Some Virtuous Desserts 205
- Some Not-So-Virtuous Desserts 207
- Two Wicked Desserts 211

INDEX 213

FOREWORD

Poets are often out of funds. Many times they try to keep body and soul together by eating candy bars, apples, doughnuts, and an occasional hamburger, usually standing up. This is a mistake. Meals should be eaten sitting down.

This book will be devoted to sitting-down meals, however humble. It will try to deal with food, however simple and inexpensive, which makes some appeal not only to taste but to sight, touch, smell, and (occasionally) hearing. Some meals will not need the aid of fire (for it is sometimes too expensive or out of reach). Others will. The simplicities of custom will sometimes be called upon; the conveniences of modern processing will also come into view.

The author realizes that other people than poets are sometimes very hard up indeed. These others (young wives and husbands making ends meet, students, musicians with uncopied scores and painters with unsold pictures, novelists in the middle of a novel, older people with small fixed stipends, and people who like to work only occasionally) may well benefit from the good sense of the following suggestions. They are offered with warm sympathy, from the wide experience of Miss Rogers and Miss Rogers' family —born and inventive cooks all.

LOUISE BOGAN

March, 1965

PREFACE TO
THE REVISED EDITION

In the baker's dozen years since *A Cookbook for Poor Poets (and Others)* was written, I have pondered basic foods, health, the energy supply, and many matters related to cooking and eating that—before—I had left to philosophers and scientists. (There is more of this in the introduction to the new chapter, "The Nickel Dinner and How It's Changed," page 175.)

Soon, in a new light, bits and pieces of the original book became dated. Some recipes no longer appealed at all. They were replaced. Others were revised and given a Roman numeral II. And, of course, there were those that were left intact.

The Revised Edition grew from scraps of paper tucked between pages, notes in margins, and manila folders when all became unwieldy.

But the original idea—the nickel dinner—remains and is offered anew for all Poor Poets (and others).

INTRODUCTION

The nickel dinner would, in periods of poverty, be gratifying indeed. Then, during those too chance bonanza moments, the same dinner could be a manifold blessing—not the least of which would be a coin or two toward the next private depression, whether it be prefaced by purchase of a painting too dear, three bars of imported soap, a box of strawberries out of season, or an unexpected tonsillectomy.

Yes, if there were truly a nickel dinner. But one can come close to this goal, not with a candy bar (for a candy bar is not really dinner) but with a big fresh roll—the French or Italian kind—the crust shattering with the first bite, the inside a network of intricate passages and domed rooms! It smells of yeast and wheatfields and waterfalls and salt flats. And because its very texture requires slow and careful munching, and each crumb must be picked up, it provides time for these natural, fragrant associations.

So this is the first rule: always have fresh bread.

The second is: always use butter.

In one period of poverty advisers noted that butter was an extravagance and that *no one* bought it. Except, perhaps, the sculptors in India who carve statues from it. Mulling over this bit of economic lore, I decided right then that I, forthwith, would always cook with butter.

The third rule: always serve wine.

There are educationally sterile methods for teaching children the days of the week. I learned Sunday first, for this was the day to go with father to buy the wine.

We brought a big empty jug and went through the Italian grocer's to the cool dim back room that was pungent with lees and oak. And over it all, the dry mustiness of vineyards in sunshine.

This was during the depression, and Sunday dinners were sometimes meager. Often they had to be stretched for friends.

But they were always gala. There was always wine. And there was always fresh bread and butter. It was, in a way, truly a nickel dinner.

And as the depression slowly recedes, so does the need for the nickel dinner. For one day there is not a rejection slip nor the refusal of a job, but a check. A small check—for it is, after all, a very small first effort.

It is now time to celebrate and to expand the menu. Or perhaps, to lay in a little store of staples.

. . .

Staples are not necessarily a sack of flour and a box of salt. Staples are whatever it is that makes the Poor Poet, and others who cook, feel secure.

There is one who says, "When I come back from Chinatown with a sack of rice, I feel secure." And another thinks, "If I had a supply of dried beans— enough to last all winter—I'm sure I'd feel a lot more secure." Yet one more announces, "I've just bought five pounds of chestnut paste. Isn't it marvelous; and it makes me feel quite well off."

And what I would want would be many shelves of herbs and spices, and a haphazard herb garden with nothing correctly labeled, and a lizard guarding it from a rock, and a kitten in drunken wantonness in the catnip. Then I, too, might feel secure.

I would have basil, bay, and marjoram; oregano, parsley, and dill; and a rosemary branch from the ceiling. I would have chervil, sage, and tarragon; savory and saffron and thyme. There would be seeds: celery, sesame, cumin, and mustard; anise, caraway, cardamom, coriander, fennel, and dill; poppy and nutmeg. Then there would be pepper, whole and ground, and allspice and cinnamon and cloves. I would have cassia buds and mace. And the chili powder and paprika and curry powder would glow in the center of it all.

I would have a tiny German nutmeg grater and a porcelain mortar and pestle. And last, and very much, a tall jar full, full, full of vanilla beans.

Then, perhaps, I would be a secure, and very rich poet.

But the truly Poor Poet must forgo this shelf. When he craves a spicy dish or heady sauce, it is often far wiser to buy pre-packaged foods than to invest in a collection of spices when only a pinch of each will be used.

The basement walls that support my house are supported in turn by the usual motley—plus a case of beautiful, if empty, wine bottles, an outgrown dog harness, and three dozen ink cans that would be fine for storage, if only there were an easy way to remove the ink—in addition to a box that illustrates the point about spices.

Acquaintances who have lived nearby, only to move on, will say, as departure approaches, "I've nowhere to pack these spices, so here. Anyway, you cook a lot."

True, but the box today contains six full tins of cayenne. Enough for a lifetime of pear and cottage cheese salads with sufficient left over to keep the cat away from the favorite plant until one or the other dies of old age. In tins full to almost empty is nutmeg to make bread pudding twice a week for eleven years. Or, if combined with the jars of whole cloves and shakers of cinnamon, pomander balls for this not too small community.

There are further treasures in the box, their full use not yet tabulated. Note, too, that although an inveterate Easter-egg maker, I have inherited such a constant rainbow of food coloring that it has been unnecessary to purchase egg dyes at any time during the past nine years.

But if the Poor Poet intends to remain in one place for any period, or is willing to take his seasonings with him, he must start his collection with little tins of these herbs and spices that only he cannot do without. Such as basil and marjoram, and rosemary and thyme.

Sliced tomatoes in summer need olive oil and basil; stewed tomatoes in winter need basil; and omelets and scrambled eggs need it.

Soups need marjoram, as do eggs when the basil runs out. And meat loaves and stews and stuffings are just meat and vegetable and bread without it.

Rosemary in wine jelly and in all meats and poultry and good thick soups.

Thyme for tomatoes and fish and meat and poultry and stews.

For spices the Poor Poet must have paprika because it's pretty and pepper because it's necessary. He must have dried mustard so he can mix his own mustard sauce to taste. Or make a poultice.

He must have cinnamon for apples and for toast. And whole cloves to chew, and nutmeg for milk punch.

Then he will need chili powder and curry powder to remind him that life is love and warm and that the sun is hot. And flour and salt and oil and wine vinegar and a wire basket of garlic. And coffee and tea.

Too, the Poor Poet needs something to cook in and something to eat from. He needs two pots and lids. Or one double boiler, for this is really three pots. He needs a frying pan with a lid and non-burnable handle, so it can go into the oven. He needs a loaf pan and a cookie sheet and a big French knife; and a wooden spoon and a fork with a long handle. And a bowl and cup and plate and glass; a knife, a fork, and spoon for each person who is going to eat.

Such was the inventory of my first "kitchen."

For although there was at last steady employment, it would be six weeks until the first check arrived. And during those forty-two days I must eat—sitting down— and so make a kitchen in the far corner that contained a wash tub for sink and a two-burner hot plate for stove.

The double boiler, a good one, was a gift, and is still in constant use. I was early to discover that one could make Poor Poet's Soufflé in the top part while heating water for tea or instant coffee in the bottom.

The frying pan was a heavy, war-surplus model that tended to rust whenever the least bit of fog blew in from Point Loma. But it was good for stews, as well as the expected frying tasks. And it led to experimentation with ovenless cookies. Because it had a metal handle, it accompanied me (rust spots and all) through a series of apartments with ovens, or sometimes not-ovens, depending on the economic status of the moment.

The loaf pan and cookie sheet came somewhat later, for without an oven their utility is questionable. Although a loaf pan is a fine place to store silverware or bits of chalk and string. Or unpaid bills.

Purchase of the French knife was, at the time, a wildly extravagant gesture. The hand-me-down hunting knife and the pocket knife, a relic of Camp Fire Girl days, did not really have to be augmented. Just yet. But ownership of a French knife became an obsession then, and there is still pride and delight in using the same knife today. So that over the years I have become firmly convinced that—if one must limit himself to one knife—this is the one to own.

It came from the best cutlery shop in San Diego. Its 10-inch blade, made of high carbon cutlery steel (not the soon-to-lose-its-fine-edge stainless), was a mere point at the end, broadening out to two inches at the base, with the steel running right through the handle, which was firmly riveted in place. It weighed over half a pound. Its manipulation was easy, and the need for the design and weight readily apparent. The pointed end was held, as though hinged, against a cutting board, and the food to be sliced was pushed under the blade. For fine chopping, the point was steadied with one hand while the other powered the knife.

This knife, because of its weight and keen blade, was also good for slicing the infrequent roast, turkey, or ham. And—although I suppose its designers never intended it—for peeling assorted fruits and vegetables, slicing bread, or splitting whole chickens.

On occasional picnics, where hot dogs were cooked on skewers fashioned from wire coat hangers, it was used to chop kindling. And, on one darkly foggy night, to pilfer bamboo for fishing poles.

The first few bowls and plates were cheap Mexican pottery that was not at all durable but was decorated in lavish, spirit-lifting colors. The cups were seconds, the work of an uninspired potter at best, and the glasses were really assorted goblets, mustard steins, and jelly jars from Goodwill.

The flatware, if it could be called that, was the remains of a family picnic set, with plastic handles (a mistake) in red, green, and yellow.

Such was the collection that, when all was ready for dinner, it proved, if nothing else, that a Poor Poet could set a colorful table—as the many ladies' magazines advise.

But more important, perhaps, was that there was fresh bread and a dish of butter. A bottle of wine, and a candle for the table.

And so the nickel dinner grew. Sometimes wildly, so that its cost was almost a dollar, this crass expenditure precipitating an abrupt return to the nickel dinner in its original form. But, between these extremes, a recipe collection began to evolve. Shoe boxes, folders, drawers held the expanding medley. When moving time came, as it did so often for so long, empty spaces in the recipe "files" were stuffed with assorted socks, soap, stamps, or screws. Again, recipes were jotted on flyleaves of books, match folders, old letters.

More than one business house has received a check along with the notation for a stew or broth scrawled on the back of the bill. During a brief stint at advertising, it was one day discovered that the recipe for Russian Pancakes had been worked out on the margin of an otherwise pristine piece of copy.

Haphazard as all this was, and still is, even with the addition at last of a neat set of filing drawers—the recipes, except for an occasional gala dish, were Poor Poet variety. And, somehow (probably because they were referred to most often), those more closely approximating the nickel dinner were filed in the front.

So it became possible, in hard times, to reach for the first card in any section and come up with a nickel dinner. Or, in affluent periods, to select something extravagant by merely reaching to the back.

And, give or take a few pennies for seasonal price fluctuations, that is how this book has been set up.

The Nickel Dinner and How It Grew

For the first expansion of the nickel dinner (which today really comes closer to twenty-five cents, considering the butter and wine) the now not so Poor Poet might consider minestrone.

It must first have been made in the country, and over a charcoal fire, with herbs and pastes and the vegetables at hand. It breathes warmth and love and vegetable rows, which belie its humble ingredients.

MINESTRONE, PIEDMONT STYLE ℛ 4

2 or 3 *small potatoes, diced*
¼ *head cabbage, shredded*
1 *large zucchini, diced*
1 or 2 *stalks celery, diced*
1½ *cups raw vegetables at hand (peas, green beans, carrots, etc., preferably fresh, not frozen)*
1 *one-pound can kidney beans*
8 *cups water*
2 *tablespoons each olive oil and butter*
½ *tablespoon dried basil leaves*
3 *cloves garlic*
¼ *teaspoon salt*
3 *tablespoons grated Parmesan cheese*

Bring the water to a boil in a large pot, dump in all the vegetables, cover and simmer for an hour. In the meantime mash together the oil, butter, basil, garlic, salt, and cheese. Just before serving, drop this paste into the soup and stir and simmer for about five minutes.

This, along with the basic nickel dinner, will serve four hungry poets, or one hungry poet and three friends.

It's to be eaten when the weather is cold and ominous and threatening. Should, however, the little check arrive on a summer day, a better choice might be a cold soup.

POOR POET'S BORSCH ❦ 4

The advantages of this soup are several-fold. It takes neither stirring nor watching over a steamy kettle, although its total effect is that it was brewed there. This, then, means that what is saved in fuel can go toward the foreseeable rainy or foggy or snowy day—paper, paint, or typewriter ribbon.

1 *one-pound can shoestring beets*
1 *10½-ounce can condensed bouillon*
2 *cups buttermilk*
3 *tablespoons brown sugar*
3 *tablespoons lemon juice*
½ *teaspoon salt*
⅛ *teaspoon pepper*
1 *tablespoon chopped onion*

Dump all the ingredients into a bowl or jar, stir well, cover, and chill thoroughly, preferably overnight.

STILL LIFE OMELET II ❦ 4–6

This is for when the first check isn't quite so small, or when a still life is being dismantled or the refrigerator cleaned. It is an elastic recipe and the vegetables can be varied with almost anything that strikes the fancy— and good taste.

STILL LIFE OMELET II

6 eggs
¼ teaspoon each basil, parsley, garlic salt, and pepper
1 cup grated cheese
3 tablespoons butter
1 large tomato, seeded and sliced
1 stalk celery, sliced
1 large zucchini, grated
1 green pepper, sliced, or leftover cooked vegetables such as asparagus, green beans, peas, spinach

Combine eggs, salt, pepper, and herbs. Add a splash of water—about 2 tablespoons. Beat in the cheese. Melt the butter in a skillet and when it begins to froth, add the eggs. Lower the heat to as low as possible. When the eggs are set but the top is still runny, sprinkle on the vegetables. (This can be done in a haphazard manner or contemplatively-creatively.)

Cut the omelet into wedges to serve, or—for a special occasion—slip the whole thing onto a platter for presentation at the table.

Don't forget the roll and butter. Or the wine.

CATS'LLEATIT

This was concocted when a bigger than expected check arrived. I was hungry for lots of meat, and the cats were, too. For, when I wandered through the kitchen to note the progress of my dinner, the cats had eaten a good share of it all up.

Cats'lleatit is manufactured from equal parts of heart, liver, tongue, kidney, sweetbreads, and/or brains (eater's choice) along with a handful each of diced salt pork and sliced onions. And a clove or two of garlic for those who like it.

Fry the salt pork. Cut the meats in small pieces and roll in flour. Brown well. Add the onion and garlic and a good shake of salt and pepper. Turn down the heat and add water to half cover the meat. Simmer, covered, for an hour, or until the meat is tender. Check the progress every so often, for the result should not be dry. Neither should it be awash. A bit of red wine, added now and then, adds to the flavor and doesn't seem to result in tipsy cats.

And, as the state of no funds at all is inevitably alleviated by the littlest check—or the biggest check ever—and back to the beginning and always, and over, and endlessly; so follow the Poor Poet's dinners.

For no matter how desperate the poet, his soul and stomach must, eventually (and preferably somewhat often), be pampered and spoiled and catered to with a really gala dinner. If only that later he can dream wistfully over his nickel dinner and through this paint or pot, or write or compose a little harder and a little better, and thus with greater, more tangible meaning and result.

For the truly gala dinner gives hope.

And the rules for hope are three: Always have something outrageously expensive. Serve it in the grandest manner. And—always use butter.

A Dinner for Instilling Hope

Such a dinner might be preceded by caviar piled on water biscuits that have been spread with soft sweet butter and Champagne cocktails in stemmed wine glasses with huge round bowls.

Sometimes my friend Nicole calls; we need, she says, an hour or so for rejuvenation. I prepare the biscuits and caviar. She arrives with a napkin-covered basket holding a split of iced Champagne, a small bottle of Cognac, maraschino cherries, and two glasses carefully wrapped in tissue.

It is a ritual, Nicole's Coupe de Champagne—a cherry and a bit of syrup in each glass, a dash of Cognac, and then the Champagne.

An hour passes. We are revivified. We know that tomorrow will be easier and that, whatever the job is, we will find a better way to do it.

So caviar with Une Coupe de Champagne is how the dinner for instilling hope should begin.

A salad next—green and crisp with only the hearts of various lettuces and a handful of water cress.

The entrée must be light: asparagus tips, perhaps, or endive or mushrooms. For what follows is something very very special.

FORREST AND SHIRLEY'S FRIED CAMEMBERT

Forrest, who—with his wife, Shirley—owns our local cheese shop, dreams up all sorts of fanciful things to do with the product he sells. There are no recipes. Rather, he outlines steps in a haphazard way—his hands doing much of the talking. His Fried Camembert is one of his prize kitchen ventures, and it goes like this:

1 *whole ripe Camembert*	*salt and pepper*
½ *cup flour*	*salad oil*
5 *tablespoons ale*	1 *jigger warmed Cognac*
1 *tablespoon raw sesame seeds*	

Make a batter of the flour, ale, sesame seeds, salt, and pepper. Heat the oil in a small skillet. There must be enough oil to half cover the Camembert. Dip the cheese into the batter. Fry quickly on both sides until puffy. Remove to a warm plate, pour the Cognac over, and ignite. Cut Fried Camembert into wedges as the flame dies.

SOUPS

The soup stone of Yeats' traveler may be the safest guide whenever the mood strikes for a pot of broth—thick or thin, hot or cold. Imagination and mystery and fancy make good soup. Renounceable here are the exact measurements and strict adherence to ingredients, paramount in the building of cakes or soufflés.

If the refrigerator affords space, a jar for collecting juices drained from vegetables, and a plastic bag for peels of carrots and potatoes (scrubbed), lettuce leaves, asparagus stems, and celery tops, is the beginning.

Tag ends of vegetables and meats can be incorporated, almost with abandon. Recalled is one superb dish whose base was French onion soup and potato salad. It has never been properly duplicated.

The remains of a bottle of white wine belong in vegetable soup or one with a poultry base. A dash of sherry goes into fish chowders, and red wine or a bit of strong coffee in soups with meat.

With boning knife and bravado, the Poor Poet can turn a pot roast of beef into steaks and soup bones; a chicken into the bases for Chicken Edgewood or Congee.

Or, if the boning knife is still being saved for, a handful of ground meat, simmered briefly and skimmed of fat, is not to be frowned upon. Nor is an appraisal of the butcher shop for lamb or chicken necks, a slice of beef heart, or even an official order of soup bones.

Insurance against want of all these, or the strength to shop, is a small store of bouillon cubes, vegetable and chicken stock bases.

Hot Soups for Cold Days

Winter reigns over the earth—a month for each of the pomegranate seeds with which Proserpina broke her fast. Often, during these months, poverty seems lurking at the heels of poets and others. It is, then, the time for hot soup in variety and abundance.

SANTAYANA'S GARLIC SOUP ⌘ 2

It was Santayana, I believe, who spoke of an excellent garlic soup his mother made. A descendant:

8 *large cloves garlic, sliced thin*
3 *or* 4 *slices French bread*
4 *tablespoons olive oil*
4 *cups water*
1 *beef bouillon cube*
4 *eggs*
½ *teaspoon salt and a little pepper*
1 *tablespoon grated Parmesan cheese*
1 *tablespoon minced parsley*

Heat half the olive oil in a saucepan and *slowly* cook the garlic until it becomes golden. Add the water and bouillon cube and simmer, covered, for 10 minutes or longer. In the meantime, fry the bread in the remaining oil and put into deep bowls, sprinkling the grated Parmesan on top. Now, poach the eggs in the soup. As soon as they are done place them on the bread slices, pour over the soup, and top with parsley.

This soup, along with a green salad, a crusty roll or two, a bit of cheese, and a bottle of red wine, is a big meal for two.

ADAM'S BREAD SOUP ↻ 2

Adam studied theology in a little summerhouse under redwood and bay and madrone. The walls were solid with books in many languages. He said they afforded insulation—from without—as this soup does from within.

4 *cups bouillon or meat stock*
2 *frankfurters, cut in pieces*
2 *poached eggs*
2 *slices toast*
   salt and pepper

Heat the frankfurters in the bouillon. Make a little arrangement of toast and egg, salt and pepper in two bowls and pour the hot soup over all.

CONGEE ↻ 4–6

Here's a good way to put to use chicken giblets, necks and backbones. Or substitute white fish or small shrimp. Congee is thick—almost a porridge. Chopped Chinese parsley, if available, is good sprinkled over. Or a little ground coriander. Sesame crackers go well on the side.

½ *pound chicken giblets*
6 *cups water*
¾ *cup raw rice*
4 *green onions, sliced*
1 *teaspoon chopped ginger root*
1 *teaspoon salt*
¼ *cup sherry*
1 *tablespoon soy sauce*
1 *large egg*

Cut giblets into small pieces. Combine all ingredients except the egg, cover and simmer 35 to 45 minutes, stirring occasionally and adding more water if necessary. When the rice has turned into a porridge, stir in a beaten egg. Serve immediately with additional soy sauce on the side.

GREEN PEA SOUP ◌ 2–4

1 *cup fresh or frozen peas*
1 *cup water*
½ *cup evaporated milk*
1 *chicken bouillon cube*
½ *teaspoon salt*
1 *canned chili pepper*

Bring water to a boil. Toss in peas, salt, bouillon cube, and the pepper, seeded and sliced. Cover and simmer 10 to 15 minutes. Add milk and heat, but do not boil, and that's all there is to it. Except, of course, for those individuals who are carried away by the Christmas spirit, and so add a plop of sour cream and a dash of cayenne or paprika to each serving.

WATER CRESS SOUP ◌ 4–6

What better reason to gather water cress on a spring day?

4 *cups water*
4 *chicken bouillon cubes*
¼ *cup shredded cooked pork or chicken*
¼ *cup finely sliced celery*
¼ *cup finely sliced water chestnuts or bamboo shoots (optional)*
2 *green onions, sliced*
1 *tablespoon soy sauce*
1 *cup chopped water cress, firmly packed*

Dissolve bouillon cubes in water and bring to boil. Add pork, celery, water chestnuts, onions, and soy. Cover and simmer 5 minutes. Increase heat, add the water cress, stir, and serve immediately.

TIN CAN CHOWDER ⌘ 4–6

An impressive dish, this chowder is ready in a half hour ... not counting the dash to the store, where French bread or pilot biscuits, red wine, and the makings for a green salad should also be procured.

4 *slices bacon*
1 *medium onion*
1 *10½-ounce can frozen potato soup or* 1 *package dehydrated type*
1 *can evaporated milk*
1 *bay leaf*
⅛ *teaspoon pepper*
1 *one-pound can salmon, shrimp, or lobster, or a combination*
½ *cup sherry*
salt to taste

Chop and sauté the bacon and onion. Add potato soup, milk, bay leaf, pepper, and fish. Cover and simmer 15 to 20 minutes. If the soup seems too thick, add a little water. Stir in sherry and salt just before serving.

SOUPAS ⌘ 10–12

The Portuguese in California celebrate the Holy Ghost Festival in early summer. Following the parade and church service, guests (and everyone is a guest, for this is what the festival is about) line up at long tables made from planks and sawhorses for a feast of soupas, bread, salad, and new wine. Then there is dancing, and more eating, and so the day goes.

Once, unable to attend the local festival, I was presented with a gallon of soupas and the following recipe.

- 5 *pounds pot roast*
- ½ *of a 3-ounce can pickling spices*
- *salt and pepper*
- ¼ *teaspoon cumin seed powder*
- 8 or 10 *stalks celery*
- 4 *large onions*
- 3 or 4 *cloves garlic*

Put the meat in a large kettle and cover with water. Cut celery, onions, and garlic in generous pieces and add, along with pickling spices tied in a cheesecloth, salt, pepper, and cumin. Cover and simmer 2 or 3 hours until the meat falls from the bones, which are then removed. Taste for seasoning. A little vinegar may be added for extra tang. Serve in large bowls along with broken pilot crackers or pieces of French bread.

Cold Soups for Hot Days

Soups from scratch: the artisanship that requires a variety of vegetables, meats, and herbs—a French knife and big wooden spoon—a large pot. These are the soups to be preferred.

But not always.

Soups made mostly from opening tins find their places. Especially on hot days.

Like the foregoing, these cold soups invite experimentation. They may be of almost any (but not every) combination. And if the weather suddenly changes, most can be transferred to the stove and served steaming.

Soups from tins can be elegant, served up in mugs, tumblers, goblets, or small bowls that can be held in the hand.

But they must be the accompaniment of fresh bread and a big pat of butter.

MADRAS ASPARAGUS ꙮ 2–3

1 *can cream of asparagus soup*
1 *soup can milk*
½ *cup plain yogurt or* 2 *tablespoons dry white wine*
   dash of salt
   curry powder to taste

Combine and mix well the soup, milk, yogurt or wine, and salt. Chill for several hours. Top each serving with a small mound of curry powder.

CHICKEN AND SESAME ꙮ 3–4

1 *can condensed cream of chicken soup*
1 *soup can milk*
1 *teaspoon soy sauce*
1 *or* 2 *tablespoons sherry*
   toasted sesame seeds

Combine and mix well the first four ingredients. Chill for several hours and pour into small bowls. Sprinkle toasted sesame seeds over each serving. A few water cress leaves, a sprig of parsley, or a pair of short pine needles (the latter not to be eaten) make a good topper.

Toast sesame seeds in a heavy pan over medium heat. It's advisable to use a lid, so that the seeds don't fly over the kitchen in the toasting process.

CELERY BRACER   2–3

1 *can cream of celery soup*
1 *soup can milk*
2 *eggs*
   dash each of salt and Tabasco
   freshly grated nutmeg

Fill a quart jar about one-third with crushed ice. Add all ingredients but the nutmeg. Fasten down the lid and shake until contents are well iced and blended. Strain, or not, into two or three tall glasses. Grate a little nutmeg over each serving.

SUMMER DAY PEA SOUP   4–6

1 *10½-ounce can condensed green pea soup*
2 *cups buttermilk*
   curry powder, toasted chopped almonds, or garlic croutons

Mix and chill well the soup and buttermilk. Serve topped with a little curry powder, almonds, or croutons.

CLIFF HANGER II   2

Purposely lacking in spirits, this brew is best on the rocks and immediately preceding the tackling of an heroic deed. Like changing a typewriter ribbon.

1 *can condensed beef broth or consommé*	*dash Tabasco*
juice of 1 *lime*	1 *cup crushed ice*

Put all the ingredients in a jar, cover, and shake well. Pour into two tall glasses and float chopped parsley or nasturtium leaves on top. If the consommé has been refrigerated, the result is truly rocky-cliff.

MARBLES ℘ 4–6

2 10½-ounce cans condensed consommé
1 4-ounce can pimientos
2 or 3 green onions
2 cups yogurt

Refrigerate the consommé well ahead so that it will jell. When ready to go, chop the pimientos and onions. Now mix everything together until the effect is that of old-fashioned marbles. This looks best served in goblets.

Don't forget a spoon. Don't let Marbles sit in the sun! And don't forget the rolls and butter! Though, in this case, toast slices, buttered, sprinkled with Parmesan, and briefly broiled, are permissible.

COLD CUCUMBER SOUP (DRINKABLE) ℘ 4

2 cups cucumbers, finely diced
1 cup chicken broth
¼ cup green onions, minced
1 stalk parsley, minced
2 cups yogurt
1 teaspoon salt
1/16 teaspoon pepper
dash Tabasco

This is easiest to make in an electric blender, but with patience and a good French knife, the vegetables can be well macerated. It should, in any case, be made a day ahead. The procedure is simply to get all the ingredients as well blended as possible and then to chill and chill.

COLD CUCUMBER SOUP (SPOONABLE) ↺ 4

3 *cups yogurt*
1 *cup water*
2 *cups finely diced cucumbers*
½ *cup currants*
½ *teaspoon dill weed*
2 *teaspoons minced mint leaves*
3 *tablespoons minced green onions*
1 *tablespoon minced parsley*
   salt and pepper

Beat the yogurt and water until smooth. Stir in the other ingredients and chill well, preferably overnight.

CHLODNIK ↺ 4

4 *cups Poor Poet's Borsch (page 9)**
½ *cup chopped cooked shrimp, ham, or veal*
1 *cucumber, diced*
1 *green onion, sliced*
4 *or 5 radishes, sliced*
2 *or 3 hard-cooked eggs, chopped*
½ *cup beet greens or spinach, shredded (optional)*
1 *small dill pickle, sliced, or 1 teaspoon dill weed*
   salt and pepper

Mix all the ingredients, chill well, and serve in soup plates. The addition of some cottage cheese will stretch the portions to include one unexpected guest.

* If it's inconvenient to make the borsch, substitute 1 quart buttermilk and 1 cup diced or shoestring beets with juice.

SALADS

The professional-type gourmet spends a lifetime crunching through an infinity of iced lettuce dressed solely with olive oil, wine vinegar, salt, and cracked pepper.

The Poor Poet may, for a time, emulate such elegance. That is, until the day the produce market is blown away by a hurricane, or truck farm crops collapse under a late snow, or rabbits get into the vegetable garden behind the house. Then, rather than risk the threat of scurvy, the Poor Poet will devise something new in the line of salads, and very good, too.

Rabbits were the instigators for most of the following.

Not-Quite Salads

SAUERKRAUT SALAD   ℘ 6–8

1 *two-pound jar sauerkraut*
3 *teaspoons salad oil*
3 *tablespoons dry white wine*
2 *teaspoons minced onion*
2 *apples*
1 *carrot*
salt and pepper

Drain and chop the kraut; toss with the oil, wine, and onion. Dice the apples and carrot and add. Season with pepper and a bit of salt. Cover and chill several hours.

This dish is not only a salad—it can serve as a relish, too. Added bits of ham or sausage turn it into a main course. And it is a great sandwich filling between slices of thickly buttered rye bread.

VEGETABLES QUO VADIS   4–6

- ¼ *cup olive oil*
- 1 *cup water*
- 2 *tablespoons wine vinegar*
- ½ *teaspoon salt*
- 4 *peppercorns*
- 2 *stalks parsley*
- ½ *teaspoon each chervil, tarragon, and thyme*
- 1 *bay leaf*
- 1 *clove garlic, mashed*
- 3 *or so cups of any or all of the following: sliced zucchini, mushrooms, diced eggplant, sliced onion, sliced carrots, asparagus stalks, celery hearts, cauliflower buds, green beans, sliced green or red peppers*

Combine all ingredients except the vegetables and bring to a boil. Add vegetables and simmer until they are barely tender. Remove vegetables and simmer the sauce until it is reduced by half. Strain it over the vegetables and chill well before serving.

This is good with, among other things, meat and cheese with crisp rolls, butter, and wine.

FRIED ZUCCHINI SALAD ↯ 6

With determination, this salad can be kept several weeks.

4 *large zucchini*	1 *large clove garlic*
flour	1 *can anchovies*
salt and pepper	*juice of 2 lemons*
¾ *cup olive oil*	1 *bunch parsley*

Cut unpeeled zucchini into ½-inch-thick rounds. Dredge them in flour, salt, and pepper and fry quickly in ¼ cup hot olive oil. They should be crisp and gold on the outside and still uncooked in the center. Drain on paper towels. Mash the other ingredients well with the remaining olive oil—more if necessary. Fill a dish with alternate layers of zucchini and anchovy-parsley sauce. Cover and chill at least 24 hours before serving.

SALSA ↯ 6–8

For years I thought this was a salad called Salsa, only to be informed recently that it's a soup called Gazpacho. But habit being what it is, it will always remain Salsa—and a salad.

½ *loaf white bread*	2 *hard-cooked eggs,*
4 *cups canned or fresh*	*chopped*
tomatoes	½ *teaspoon salt*
1 *clove garlic, mashed*	¼ *teaspoon pepper*
1 *onion, chopped*	1½ *teaspoons Worcester-*
4 *stalks celery, chopped*	*shire*
1 *green pepper, chopped,*	*dash Tabasco*
seeds removed	8 *tablespoons olive oil*
1 *small cucumber, chopped*	4 *tablespoons wine vinegar*
1 *can green chilies, chopped*	*or lemon juice*

Soak bread in water, drain and mash with the tomatoes. Dump in all other ingredients, stir nicely, and let chill for a minimum of 4 hours. Stir well again before serving. The absent-minded poet, who forgets to add the celery, green pepper, onion, and chilies, will come up with an excellent, though less fiery Salsa.

WINTER PEARS ∽ 4

Sometimes everything that might logically make a salad is out of season. Sometimes a change of pace is called for. And, sometimes, one is presented with a whole box of pears. Here is one way to go.

4 *pears*
1 *lemon*
2 *tablespoons* each *capers, chopped pimiento,*
minced parsley, and chopped green onion
$\frac{1}{4}$ *cup white wine vinegar*
salt

Core and slice the pears. Slice the lemon paper-thin. Add the other ingredients, stir gently, cover, and chill.

Serve Winter Pears in goblets or wine glasses as an appetizer, on a bit of lettuce as a salad, or simply pass the bowl around as a "side dish" if it's chicken or ham for dinner.

Hungry Poet Salads

When the weather's too hot, or the fuel bill has been too high, or there isn't a stove at all, it's good to have big, full-meal salads. More dignified than eating something from a can and less extravagant than picking up bits and pieces from the delicatessen.

In any case, the crisp roll and butter, and wine add infinite pleasure.

ARTISTS' SPECIAL ↻ 2–4

1 *pint cottage cheese*
¼ *cup mayonnaise*
2 *tablespoons prepared horse-radish*
3 *green onions, chopped*
   salt and pepper
   lettuce, broken fairly small

Toss everything but the lettuce gently and patiently with a fork, and then plop on 3 or 4 plates well-piled with lettuce. If there's not enough lettuce, use some chopped raw spinach. And if there's neither lettuce nor spinach, eat as is.

A WAGNERIAN SALAD ↻ 4–6

3 *cups diced cooked beef,*
   veal, ham, or tongue
2 *dill pickles*
1 *medium onion, sliced*
1 *tablespoon capers*
1 *tablespoon minced parsley*

1 *teaspoon prepared*
   German mustard
1 *medium boiled potato,*
   diced
   salt and pepper

MARINADE

2 *tablespoons olive oil*
3 *tablespoons vinegar*

3 *tablespoons cold beef*
   stock

Toss together the salad ingredients. Mix the marinade and add. Cover and chill for several hours.

CABBAGE AND PEANUTS   4–5

2 cups shredded cabbage
1 firm pear, cored and diced
3 tablespoons chopped salted peanuts
1 tablespoon cider vinegar
½ teaspoon celery salt
6 tablespoons sour cream

Toss all ingredients and chill before serving. This is also good hot, served with mashed potatoes. In this case, steam the cabbage until it is just wilted and then toss with other ingredients.

WALNUTS AND RICE   6

4 cups leftover rice
1 cup chopped celery
1 cup chopped toasted walnuts
¼ cup sliced pimiento-stuffed green olives
2 tablespoons finely chopped onion
½ teaspoon oregano
½ teaspoon grated lemon peel
¼ cup salad oil
2 tablespoons lemon juice
salt and pepper
yogurt

Stir everything together except the yogurt, and pile into a serving dish or into a container to carry to a picnic. The yogurt? A spoonful of *that* tops each serving.

PICNIC SALAD   4

1 head lettuce, broken
1 tin anchovy fillets
1 or 2 hard-cooked eggs
1 or 2 lemons
salt, pepper, and garlic

This is ideally suited for a picnic, for all ingredients are carried separately and mixing is done on the spot as follows: open anchovy tin and cut the fillets into short pieces, being careful not to lose any oil. Peel the eggs and cut them into the lettuce. Now dump in the tin of anchovies and their oil; salt, pepper, and garlic to taste; and squeeze over the juice of the lemons. Combine well and serve along with hunks of French bread and plenty of dry red wine.

VINTNERS' POTATO SALAD ଓ 8

In the hills of Berkeley is an old redwood house with a shower stall made from a telephone booth—intact except for the phone itself. On Telegraph Hill across the Bay is one made from a large wine vat. And this recipe for the owner's special potato salad.

2½ *pounds potatoes*
1 *cup dry white wine*
4 *hard-cooked eggs, chopped*
2 *stalks celery, chopped*
1 *onion, chopped*
2 *tablespoons capers*
2 *tablespoons chopped parsley*

1 *tablespoon celery seed*
1 *tablespoon seasoning salt*
½ *teaspoon pepper*
4 *tablespoons French dressing*
¼ *cup each mayonnaise and sour cream*

Boil or bake the potatoes until tender, peel them, and slice into a bowl. Pour the wine over the hot potatoes and let sit for about an hour. In the meantime, mix together all other ingredients and, hoping the potatoes are still somewhat warm, fold the sauce into them. The result should not be mashed potato salad. Chill well for several hours before serving.

The potato salad addict might like a change now and then, and so substitute dill weed and a little chopped pickle or olives for the capers; or use caraway instead of celery seed.

POET'S SALAD FROM THE EAST ♋ 6

White wine and warm flour tortillas with the salad; fruit, cookies, and tea later. An entire meal.

$\frac{1}{2}$ *pound bean sprouts*
2 *or* 3 *cups shredded left-over beef, ham, or chicken, or cubed soybean curd*
$\frac{1}{4}$ *head lettuce, shredded*
3 *or* 4 *green onions, chopped*
$\frac{1}{2}$ *cup chopped fresh coriander*
$\frac{1}{3}$ *cup parched sesame seeds*
$\frac{1}{4}$ *cup sesame oil*
4 *tablespoons vinegar*
2 *tablespoons soy sauce*
$\frac{1}{2}$ *teaspoon Five Fragrant Spices (See* Chinese Five Spices, page 202.)
pepper

Just toss everything together, pile into bowls, and serve. If this is going on an outing, carry the dressing (the last five ingredients) separately. Bean sprouts tend to "melt"—fast.

VEGETABLES IN SANDALS

This is pleasant to eat while wearing sandals and sitting in the sun. Good music, red wine, crisp rolls and butter complete this pastorale.

small tomatoes, quartered
boiled potatoes, sliced
green beans, cooked tender-crisp
several slices red onion, separated into rings
green pepper slices
cauliflower buds, cooked tender-crisp
pitted black olives
anchovy fillets
small can tuna
1 *or* 2 *hard-cooked eggs, quartered*
dressing of red wine vinegar, olive oil, Dijon mustard, salt, and pepper

Chill the vegetables, fish, and eggs and just before serving toss with the dressing. The whole is elegant served on a foundation of French bread slices or pilot biscuits.

Four Necessary Dressings

Three for *green* salads (head lettuce, romaine, spinach, water cress, and the like) and one for fruit, these dressings are as necessary to the salad tosser as a tube of white lead and a can of turpentine are to the painter.

Three rules for really good green salads: Have the greens and the salad bowl terribly cold. If not using a prepared-in-advance dressing, be sure to add oil first and vinegar the very last. Never, never combine the greens and dressing until the very moment of eating.

BIG SUR DRESSING   ℭ 2 cups

$\frac{3}{4}$ *cup Japanese rice vinegar*
$\frac{3}{4}$ *cup chopped parsley*
1 *green onion*
1 *slice fresh ginger root*
3 *tablespoons brown sugar*
$\frac{1}{8}$ *teaspoon salt*
$\frac{1}{4}$ *teaspoon MSG*
$\frac{3}{4}$ *cup buttery oil*
$\frac{1}{4}$ *cup olive oil*

Peel the ginger root, chop the onion, and place all ingredients in a blender. Blend until you have a frothy green dressing which, when refrigerated, will keep three weeks.

KATHA'S SALAD DRESSING   ℭ 2 cups

1 *cup red wine vinegar*
1 *cup olive oil*
2 *tablespoons raw sugar*
2 *cloves garlic, cut up*
$\frac{1}{2}$ *teaspoon salt*
$\frac{1}{2}$ *teaspoon coarse ground pepper*
$\frac{1}{2}$ *teaspoon curry powder*
1 *teaspoon dried tarragon or oregano or dill*

Place the ingredients in a container with a tight lid. Shake well. In fact, shake the jar whenever you pass. This dressing is *not to be refrigerated.*

BLUE CHEESE DRESSING ℭ 1 cup

This keeps well in the refrigerator. It's good to make when a long-forgotten and somewhat strong hunk of blue cheese finally comes to light in the far reaches of the cooler.

$\frac{1}{2}$ *cup crumbled blue cheese*
$\frac{1}{2}$ *cup salad oil*
$\frac{1}{4}$ *plus cup wine vinegar*
salt and pepper to taste
dash of cayenne

Mash cheese and oil with a fork. Add the vinegar, a little at a time, while stirring. Season to taste.

BRENDA'S HEAVY FRENCH DRESSING ℭ 2 cups

Particularly good with citrus salads, grapefruit and avocado, or sliced oranges and sweet onions, this is another dressing *not to be refrigerated.*

$\frac{1}{3}$ *cup powdered sugar*
1 *teaspoon dry mustard*
$\frac{1}{2}$ *teaspoon mustard seed*
$\frac{1}{4}$ *teaspoon paprika*
$\frac{1}{4}$ *teaspoon salt*
$\frac{1}{8}$ *teaspoon cayenne*
$\frac{1}{8}$ *teaspoon black pepper*
$\frac{1}{3}$ *cup chili sauce*
1 *teaspoon grated onion*
$\frac{1}{3}$ *cup red wine vinegar*
$\frac{2}{3}$ *cup salad oil*

Mix dry ingredients, add chili sauce and onion. Combine oil and vinegar and stir in slowly.

BUILDING WITH EGGS AND CHEESE

No hen will lay her eggs for you
Unless they're placed in baskets, too.
—HAROLD LEWIS

Eggs, one of the most useful of the food products, are of infinite value to the Poor Poet. Not only are they necessary in a number of dishes as binder, clarifier, stabilizer, leavener, and garnish; but they may be served up almost as is for any meal during the day. Or night. And they look nice in a straw basket.

And, for the nutritionally minded, they are one of the few complete foods.

Not counting the Chinese method of preparing thousand-year eggs (which now, thanks to a new process, can be made "instantly") there are about a dozen approved egg cookery methods. But, for the Poor Poet, we stick primarily to scrambling or omelet methods—for their economic virtues alone.

Ways with Eggs

BAREFOOT OMELET   ❧ 4

If a cup or two of cold cooked spaghetti or noodles is substituted for the potatoes, this becomes Shoestring Omelet. So named in honor of the local poets who were recently apprised of the fact that it is against the law to run around in bare feet.

2 *tablespoons butter or olive oil*
2 *boiled potatoes, sliced*
4 *eggs*
2 *tablespoons milk*
1 *tablespoon grated dry cheese*
   salt and pepper

Brown the potatoes in butter. Beat eggs with milk, cheese, salt and pepper, and pour over the potatoes. Cook slowly, about 5 minutes on each side, or—if the flipping-over process is impracticable, proceed as for scrambled eggs.

Those who wish to spend the next several hours alone may add garlic to taste.

EGGS FOR A SUMMER MORNING ✣ 2

4 *eggs*   *salt*
1 *cup sour cream or*   *freshly ground pepper*
   yogurt

Prepare soft-boiled eggs that are on the firm side. Peel while hot and drop into two bowls of sour cream or yogurt. Add a bit of salt—lots of pepper.

HYPNOTIC EYES

Although its creator claims this composition was designed primarily for laughs, it's good for a crowd or for buffet service. For each person:

2 *slices bread*   2 *eggs*
1 *tablespoon butter*   1 *tablespoon grated cheese*
4 *tablespoons cream*   *salt, pepper, and paprika*

Remove the centers of the bread (use them later for Down and Out Eggs or for Bread Pudding) and brown the part that's left in butter. Sprinkle a baking dish with a little cream, lay in the bread rounds, and break a raw egg in the center of each slice. Sprinkle on the cheese and seasonings and a bit more cream. Bake in a moderate (350°) oven about 15 minutes, or until the eggs are set.

STEAMED EGGS ☙ 3–4

Handy for when there's only enough butter for the fresh rolls.

6 *eggs*	1 *tablespoon sherry*
1 *tablespoon soy sauce*	1 *3½-ounce can mushrooms*

Beat the eggs with the soy and sherry. Pour into the top of a double boiler that has been wiped with a little oil. Cover and steam until the eggs are almost set. Stir in the mushrooms and continue cooking until done.

DOWN AND OUT EGGS ☙ 4–6

A *big* breakfast as well as a boon to the one hot plate cooking setup.

- ¼ *pound bacon, diced (or leftover ham, luncheon meat, bologna)*
- 4 *eggs*
- 12 *crackers, crushed*
- ¼ *cup milk or water*
- 2 *tablespoons chopped onion*
-   *salt and pepper*
- 6 *slices bread*
-   *grated cheese (optional)*

Fry bacon until it is crisp. Meanwhile make a thin batter of the eggs, crackers, milk, salt, and pepper. Without draining the fat from the pan, sprinkle in the onions, cover the bottom of the pan with bread, and pour over the egg mixture. Cook for about 10 minutes over low heat; flip the whole thing over and continue cooking until the eggs are set. Sprinkle the grated cheese over just after the flipping.

HUEVOS RANCHEROS

This is an eye-opener from Ensenada where we once befriended a poet awaiting a long overdue fruit boat and points south. In the evenings we had tequila and limes for a dime, and in the mornings platters of huevos rancheros and big glasses of orange juice. For each serving:

3 *tortillas*
2 *eggs*
½ *cup enchilada sauce*
   Mexican hot sauce or Tabasco

Heat the tortillas in the top of a double boiler, or fry lightly, and place on a plate. Fry the eggs and slip them on top of the tortillas. Drown each serving in steaming hot enchilada sauce. Extra hot sauce is for the braver fire eaters.

SCRAMBLED EGGS WITH ℧ 4
CURRY AND BLACK BUTTER

6 *eggs, well beaten*
1 *teaspoon curry powder*
¼ *teaspoon salt*
6 *tablespoons cream*
4 *slices bacon, diced*
1 *small onion, chopped fine*
½ *green pepper, chopped fine, seeds removed*
¼ *cup butter*

Dissolve the curry powder and salt in the cream and add to beaten eggs. Fry bacon until crisp, then sauté onion and pepper. Discard any excess fat and pour egg mixture into pan. Scramble slowly. Meanwhile, brown the butter in a saucepan and pour a little over each serving of eggs.

EGGS WITH BLACK BEANS   ↻ 6

2 *tablespoons salad oil*	½ *soup can water*
1 *clove garlic, minced*	2 *tablespoons butter*
1 *large onion, chopped fine*	6 *eggs*
¾ *cup stewed tomatoes*	½ *cup grated cheese*
1 *can condensed black bean soup*	*salt and pepper*

Sauté the garlic and onion in oil until vegetables are light brown. Add the tomatoes, bean soup, and water; mix well and simmer for 10 minutes or so. Butter a large flat baking dish and break the eggs into it. Sprinkle them with salt, pepper, and cheese and spread the bean mixture on top. Dot with more butter and bake in a 375° oven until the eggs are set.

Serve with hot crisp rolls or steamed tortillas and butter.

Omelets

After Easter is a good time for omelets, the pre-holiday weeks having involved daily scrambled eggs so that enough shells can be blown clean for decorating and giving away. So far no acceptable method has been devised for blowing eggs and coming out with yolks and whites neatly separated.

'06 OMELET ℭ 4

Like Caruso this omelet did not really survive the San Francisco earthquake. Devised some years later, it takes its name from the fact, however, that had it been in the quake, it would no doubt have come through its puffy, light self. Unless a brick toppled on it.

4 *eggs, separated*
2 *tablespoons water*
2 *tablespoons flour*
½ *teaspoon salt*
⅛ *teaspoon pepper*
1 *tablespoon butter*

Eggs should be at room temperature to insure a successful omelet. Beat the whites and salt until stiff. Combine and beat the other ingredients (except butter) and fold most gently into the egg whites. Melt the butter in a big iron skillet over a low fire and pour in the batter. Cover the skillet and let cook for about 12 minutes. Now uncover the pan and put it into a slow oven to set the top. Slide the omelet out onto a warm plate, fill it with anything that seems reasonable, and serve to four.

Reasonable fillings run from the usual creamed vegetables and meats to cottage cheese, chili beans, canned spaghetti, undiluted gumbo soup, or fried potatoes with lots of onions and a wash of cream.

FOUR-HANDED OMELET ℭ 4–5

1 *tablespoon butter*
½ *pound boned chicken breasts or lean pork*
¼ *cup chopped roasted peanuts*
1 *clove garlic, pressed*
4 *green onions, sliced*
1½ *tablespoons soy sauce*
pinch of sugar
pepper

For this omelet two cooks are better than one, for the '06 Omelet and the filling are best prepared at the same time. But it can be managed alone if the mind is not allowed to wander.

Cut the meat in tiny pieces and sauté in butter. Add the remaining ingredients and cook and stir just to heat well.

THE SPOILED LOVER   ଦ 4

Well, why not? This calls for a dimly lighted room and grandmother's chafing dish—or some agile footwork between stove and table.

Prepare the standby '06 Omelet, this time flavoring it with $\frac{1}{4}$ cup powdered sugar and $\frac{1}{2}$ teaspoon vanilla. In a separate pan heat a jar of preserved mixed fruits, the juice thickened with a big spoonful of apricot jam and a little cornstarch. In yet another pan heat $\frac{1}{2}$ cup rum or brandy.

When ready for the finale, slip the omelet onto a large plate, pile the fruit around, sprinkle with a little sugar, pour the warm rum over the fruit, and ignite. When the flame begins to flicker the omelet is ready to serve.

Dishes Incorporating Both Eggs and Cheese

POOR POET'S SOUFFLÉ I   ଦ 6

Although not a soufflé in the true sense of the word, this (and Soufflé II) is less traumatic for the nervous cook than is the genuine thing. Besides, it will turn out, in almost the worst of ovens.

    12 *slices stale bread*
    butter
    2 *cups cottage cheese*
    1 *teaspoon horse radish*
    4 *eggs*
    2¼ *cups milk*
    ½ *teaspoon salt and some pepper*

Butter both the bread slices and a baking dish large enough to hold 6 slices laid flat. Stir horse radish into the cottage cheese and spread over the slices. Top with other slices, buttered on both sides, if possible. Beat remaining ingredients and pour over the bread. Let stand about 30 minutes. Bake for 30 to 40 minutes at 350°.

Last night's garlic bread makes a terrific soufflé. In this case, cut down on or completely omit the horseradish, using instead additional crushed garlic.

POOR POET'S SOUFFLÉ II   ℭ 6

    12 *slices stale bread*
    ½ *pound sharp cheese, sliced or grated*
    2 *large onions*
    6 *eggs*
    2 *cups milk*
    ½ *teaspoon each salt and dry mustard and some pepper*

Build 2 layers of bread, cheese, and sautéed onions in a buttered baking dish. Beat the eggs, milk, and seasonings and pour over the bread. Let stand for an hour, then bake in a 300° oven for 45 minutes.

Rye bread with Swiss cheese is interesting. So is the addition of bacon, ham, or chipped beef. Caraway or poppy seeds add variety. And ¼ cup sherry in place of an equal quantity of milk is hardly to be frowned upon.

PRAGMATIC PIZZA

Here, the quantity of ingredients is dependent upon the appetites of the eaters.

French bread, sliced
garlic
olive oil
cottage cheese
paprika

Generously anoint French bread slices with garlic, then lay each slice in a baking pan covered with olive oil to about $\frac{1}{8}$ inch. Spread cottage cheese over the bread and sprinkle on a bit of paprika. Bake in a 375° oven until the cheese is bubbly, and prepare to eat immediately. A big green salad, perhaps with anchovies, and lots of red wine round out the menu.

ALPINE PIE ℧ 6

1 *9-inch unbaked pie shell*
12 *slices bacon*
1 *onion*
$\frac{1}{2}$ *cup shredded Swiss cheese*
1 *tablespoon flour*
3 *eggs*
1 *cup milk*
2 *tablespoons chopped parsley*
dash Worcestershire sauce
salt and pepper

Fry the bacon, removing six slices when they are partially cooked and six when they are crisp. Chop the onion, sauté it in 2 tablespoons bacon drippings, and spoon it into the pie shell. Sprinkle the cheese, then the flour on top. Beat the eggs, stir in the crisp bacon—crumbled—milk, and seasonings. Pour into pie shell. Arrange the partially cooked bacon on top, forming spokes, so that the pie resembles an edible wagon wheel. Bake 15 minutes at 400°, then 25 minutes at 300°. When a knife inserted in the center comes out clean, the pie is ready to eat.

CHEESE PIE, LEFT BANK 4–6

1 *9-inch unbaked pastry shell*
2 *cups cottage cheese*
2/3 *cup sour cream*
2 *cups mashed potatoes*
2 *eggs, well beaten*
1 *teaspoon salt*
3 *tablespoons onion, chopped*
3 *tablespoons pimiento or pimiento-stuffed green olives, chopped*
1½ *tablespoons butter*

Blend cottage cheese with sour cream. Beat in the potatoes and then all other ingredients except the butter. Use this to dot the top of the filling after it is poured into the pastry shell. Bake at 350° for 1 to 1¼ hours, or until filling is set.

Although this cheese pie is better hot, it is quite good cold, and so an excellent main dish for a picnic.

SPINACH PIEROGI 4–6

A big platter of Pierogi is superb, especially on a cool night. But the cottage cheese must be well drained or the dish is guaranteed to fall apart at least twice: once while being rolled on the floured board and again while simmering.

1 *bunch spinach*	1 *cup Parmesan cheese*
1 *tablespoon butter*	1 *cup flour*
1 *pint dry cottage cheese*	*salt, pepper, and*
2 *eggs*	*nutmeg*

Chop—veritably mince—the spinach and wilt it in butter over low heat. Combine with the cottage cheese, eggs, half the Parmesan, ½ cup flour, and the seasonings. Chill for several hours. Roll walnut-sized Pierogi on a well-floured board. Cook a few at a time in gently boiling water—10 minutes is safe. Remove with a slotted spoon to a large platter and sprinkle with more cheese.

TOPFENKNÖDEL ℭ 4

This cheese dumpling from Czechoslovakia may be served either as a main dish or as a dessert, or even a breakfast dish.

1 *pound dry cottage cheese*
2 *slices bread, soaked in water and drained*
2 *egg yolks*
1 *tablespoon flour*
2 *tablespoons bread crumbs*
½ *teaspoon salt*

Mix all ingredients well and set in refrigerator for an hour. Shape the dough into dumplings and dust with flour. Drop the dumplings into boiling salted water or stock, and boil gently for 5 to 10 minutes. Remove with a slotted spoon. Serve sprinkled with sugar and cinnamon and hot melted butter poured over all. Or serve as a soup along with the stock in which they were cooked.

RUSSIAN PANCAKES ℭ 4

Easier than blintzes, and almost as good.

1½ *pounds cottage cheese*
2 *egg yolks*
1 *whole egg*
½ *cup flour*
  butter
1 *quart, at least, sour cream*

Drain cottage cheese in a cheesecloth-lined sieve or colander. This takes overnight. Now, working with a large bowl, not the colander, beat in the yolks and whole egg and blend in the flour. Chill well, form into cakes no more than ½ inch thick, roll in flour or fine crumbs, and fry until golden-brown in lots of butter. Serve topped with mounds of sour cream.

SWISS EGGS ❧ 6

An ode to the mountains? Swiss Eggs is in keeping with such a worthy endeavor.

2 cups grated Swiss cheese	*salt and pepper*
6 tablespoons butter	*pinch of nutmeg*
1½ cups dry white wine	*6 eggs*
1 teaspoon each chopped parsley, chervil, thyme, and shallots	*6 slices toast anchovy paste*

Put cheese, half the butter, the wine, and the seasonings into a heavy skillet. Turn the heat to the very lowest while separating the eggs and beating the whites until stiff. Now give all attention to the cheese, which is slowly melting. Stir constantly until it begins to bubble. Beat in yolks one at a time. Add the whites, and scramble well but gently.

Pile the eggs on toast spread with butter and a bit of anchovy paste.

This is a rich dish that calls for a tossed green salad and white wine. Or, if eaten at breakfast, fresh fruit and lots of strong coffee.

FRIED CREAM CHEESE   4–6

Here is a sophisticated version of the Monterey fishermen's delight. Their method is simply to take squares of very soft Jack or Tillamook cheese, roll it in crumbs, and fry in hot olive oil in which many cloves of garlic are bubbling. The cheese is eaten along with French bread, cold vegetables or a green salad, and wine.

2 *eggs*
3 *egg yolks*
1 *cup plus 2 tablespoons flour*
¼ *teaspoon salt*
  pepper and a little nutmeg
1 *cup grated Swiss cheese*
1 *quart milk*
  fine bread or cracker crumbs
  oil for frying

Warm the milk. In the meantime, beat the eggs in the top of a double boiler. (Remember—lightly beaten eggs thicken better.) Alternately blend in the flour and milk. Stir in the salt, pepper, and nutmeg. Place the mixture over gently boiling water and allow to thicken while stirring constantly. Indispensable here: a wire whisk and patience. In about 10 minutes, when the mixture is the consistency of a thick white sauce, remove it from the heat, stir in the cheese, and turn it into a well-buttered pan. Cover and chill well.

When serving time comes, cut the cheese into inch-thick slices, dip in crumbs (dipping first into slightly beaten egg white makes a lighter crust), and fry quickly in hot oil. Garlic lovers are urged to toss several cloves of that bulb into the oil.

BEANS, PEAS, RICE, AND ASSORTED CEREALS

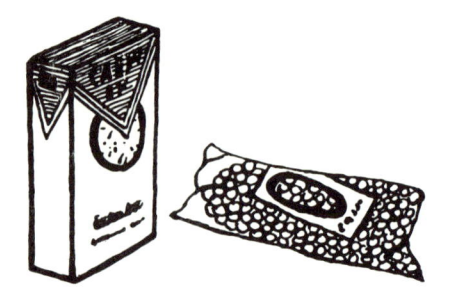

Venus gave Psyche three tasks to prove that she was deserving of Cupid's love. First, she was to separate into individual heaps an enormous storehouse of seeds of all kinds—wheat, beans, lentils, poppy, barley, and many others.

Although cereals are no longer piled in such slipshod fashion and, moreover, can rarely be bought in bulk from big sacks and boxes heaped along the wall, it is still best to sort through for an odd weed seed or pebble should one deserve love. A well-cooked and seasoned pebble under a new inlay can dampen romance.

For the non-bean-sorter, the person who doesn't like to cook from scratch—or doesn't have the time, or the money for fuel—there are more ready-to-eat concoctions on the market than there were kinds of seeds in Psyche's task. Some are quite good, but usually expensive. But any of them can be improved with tampering.

Catsup, mustard, molasses, cut-up ham, frankfurters or bacon, and a dash of strong black coffee, red wine, or rum are standbys.

Bean Dishes from Canned Beans

FIREBAUGH BEANS ℧ 2

Firebaugh was a dusty farm labor town in the San Joaquin Valley when a young and unsuccessful writer lived primarily on this dish—which is good.

1 *one-pound can pork and beans (remove pork)*
1 *medium onion, chopped*
1 *large tomato, chopped*
salt and pepper

That's all. Mix it and eat it, although chilling for a few hours does improve the flavor.

CONDÉ ℧ 2–4

¼ *pound bacon, diced*
4 *green onions, chopped*
2 *bay leaves*
salt and pepper
1 *#2½ can kidney beans*
½ *cup evaporated milk*
1 *cup hot water*
¼ *teaspoon gumbo filé powder*

Brown bacon and onion and add all ingredients except the filé powder. Cook over low heat for 15 minutes. Stir in filé powder and serve in bowls with crisp rolls and butter and a big green salad.

GRANT AVENUE BEANS ℧ 6

This can be all mixed together and either heated well for winter eating or chilled for summer. Or eat it cold any time and save on the fuel bill.

2 *one-pound cans kidney beans, drained*
1 *clove garlic, crushed*
3 *tablespoons olive oil*
½ *cup red wine*
2 *tablespoons minced parsley*
½ *cup chopped olives*
salt and pepper

ARTISTS' BAKED BEANS ೞ 2

Another hot-or-cold concoction for two hungry artists.

1 *one-pound can baked beans*
1 *teaspoon prepared mustard*
2 *tablespoons chili sauce*
1 *cup cottage cheese*
½ *cup chopped onions*
1 *tablespoon minced parsley*

Mix together the first 3 ingredients and heat well. Dump into a deep dish and top with the cottage cheese, onion, and parsley, in that order. For hot weather eating, skip fussing over the stove by mixing and chilling all ingredients.

COUNTRY MOUSE BEANS ೞ 4

"Better beans and bacon in peace than cakes and ale in fear," says Aesop's Country Mouse to his cousin. This is good for feeding visiting city mice, among others.

1 *large onion, chopped*
butter
½ *cup green peppers, chopped, seeds removed*
½ *cup diced ham*
1 *can Italian tomato paste*
1 *cup red wine*
2 *#2 cans baked kidney beans*
8 *strips bacon*

Sauté the onion, pepper, and ham in a little butter. Add the tomato paste and wine and cook and stir about 5 minutes. Dump in the beans and stir briefly before turning the mixture into a casserole. Lay the bacon over the top and bake for 30 minutes at 350°. This, along with hard rolls, green salad, and the rest of the wine, will please four city mice, with some left over for the cook.

BEANS FOR A HOT OR COLD NIGHT ↻ 4–6

1 *large onion, chopped*
1 *tablespoon butter*
¼ *pound mushrooms, sliced*
2 *#2 cans pinto or small red beans*
1 *small can chopped green chilies*

Sauté the onion, add the mushrooms and, in a minute or so, the drained beans and the chilies. Cover and simmer for 10 minutes. A warmer-upper when the rain is beating on a roof that may or may not be leaking; a bracer-upper when the sun is pouring through un-insulated walls.

BEANS WITH ORANGES ↻ 4

Bad luck to misplace this dish in the far reaches of the refrigerator, for such action would make the cook a wrongdoer, and thus punishable by the speaking beans of folklore, which existed solely to mete out punishments. And, more to the point, the oranges will become limp.

1 *large orange*
1 *one-pound can pork and beans*
1 *one-pound can kidney beans*
2 *tablespoons orange marmalade*
1 *teaspoon dry mustard*
½ *pound cut-up ham, sausage, or crisp bacon*

Grate a bit of rind from each end of the orange. Cut the rest in thin slices and reserve. Drain the beans and combine with the grated rind and other ingredients in a baking dish. Arrange the orange slices over the beans, cover the dish, and bake at 375° for 30 minutes. There's quite an interesting taste-texture experience if the orange (skin and all) is cut in bite-size pieces and stirred gently into the beans about 5 minutes before serving.

GUMBO BEANS AND SAUSAGE 6–8

1 *onion, chopped*
1 *tablespoon bacon fat*
2 *one-pound cans pink beans*
½ *teaspoon dry mustard*
1 *can chicken gumbo soup*
1½ *cups canned tomatoes*
6 *frankfurters, sliced*

Brown the onion in the fat. Drain the beans (save the liquid) and add, along with all the other ingredients. Stir to mix, cover the pot, and let simmer gently for a half hour or so. Stir every so often and add a little bean liquor if the mixture seems dry. Serve with rice and brown bread.

WESTERN CHILI 8–12

Joseph P. MacCarthy noted that, to be happy in New England, one must make sure in advance that his obituary appears in the *Boston Transcript*—and, eat beans on Saturday night.

The western version of a Boston Saturday night is chili. It's eaten in the kitchen in winter and in the patio in summer. Great kettles of it are lugged to the mountains or the desert or the shore. Or to an ailing friend whose digestive tract is still in order.

1 *pound ground beef*
1 *large onion, chopped*
1 *clove garlic, mashed*
1 *green pepper, chopped, seeds removed*
2 *one-pound cans red beans*
1 *#2½ can tomatoes*
1 *cup tomato juice*
2 *bouillon cubes*
½ *teaspoon each basil, oregano, cumin, and thyme*
1 *tablespoon chili powder, or more to taste*
1 *cup chopped ripe olives salt to taste*

Brown the beef in a little oil, adding the onion, garlic, and pepper when the meat is about half done. Dump everything into a large kettle and simmer, covered, at least an hour. If the chili is made ahead and reheated, it's better. Look, sniff, taste, and stir from time to time, and see that the mixture doesn't get too dry. In which case add coffee in preference to water.

This is a no-panic recipe, for the ingredients can be varied every which way. Furthermore, it will feed up to twelve if it's served over macaroni, rice, or corn chips. A BIG green salad is called for, as well as hard rolls and red wine.

Bean Dishes from Dried Beans

Dried bean cooking is for not-so-Poor Poets who don't shudder at utility bills. It is necessary for those who receive a sack of beans at Christmas.

So all the preceding canned bean dishes can be made from scratch although it takes longer. Cooking time is decreased somewhat if a spoonful of unseasoned meat tenderizer is added to the overnight soak.

Here, however, are two elegant dried bean dinners that must be made from scratch and then only if black beans can be located. A Mexican or Chinese grocer is the best target. Black beans look like little blobs of India ink; they have a strong and wild flavor; they cost anywhere from twenty cents to a dollar a pound. They require at least three hours' cooking and sometimes costly ingredients. But the final product is superb.

BLACK BEANS AND RUM ℞ 8

1 *pound black beans*	1 *ham hock or small ham bone*
1 *medium onion*	
½ *bay leaf*	3 *dashes Tabasco*
⅛ *teaspoon thyme*	½ *teaspoon salt*
1 *large stalk celery*	¼ *cup Jamaica rum*
2 *branches parsley*	1½ *pints cold sour cream*

Sort the beans (leave one white one in for good luck) and soak overnight. Drain, cover with fresh water, add the next 6 ingredients, and simmer, covered, 2½ to 3 hours. Pick out the vegetables and ham hock and drain the beans, reserving the liquid. Thicken a cup of it with little kneaded butter-flour balls, and return it to the beans along with the Tabasco, salt, and rum. Reheat and serve with gobs of sour cream, French bread and butter, red wine, and an enormous green salad.

BLACK BEANS WITH SMOKED MEATS ℞ 12

This variation on a Brazilian national dish is good for winding up the day, any day, or celebrating in the grand manner.

1 *pound black beans*
2 *pounds smoked meats (about equal parts of corned beef, smoked sausage, smoked pork, smoked tongue, and bacon)*
1 *large onion, chopped*
3 *green onions, chopped*
1 *clove garlic, mashed*
4 *tablespoons bacon fat or oil*
   dash of cayenne
   salt to taste

Check the beans for assorted rocks and weed seeds and soak overnight. Or cover the beans with cold water, bring to a boil and boil several minutes, then allow to stand for an hour. Drain the beans, cover with fresh water, and simmer for 2 hours. In the meantime, simmer meats in a separate pan.

Drain the meat, reserving some liquid for possible later use, should the final result seem dry; peel the tongue and slice it, along with the other meats. Add meat to beans and continue cooking slowly until the beans are soft enough that some of them can be mashed.

Now sauté the onions in the fat, add the garlic and cayenne, and mix with the beans. Taste for seasoning, and the dish is ready to serve. Piles of steamed rice are a must. Twelve persons can eat this in one day, or one person in twelve days.

Jamaica rum or strong black coffee added now and then during the cooking does not hinder the dish one bit.

Black beans are to be more than briefly noted—never ignored. In the Roman midnight observation that closed the three-day Lemuria, or entertainment of the dead, the head of the household walked barefoot through all his rooms, throwing black beans behind him. His chant, repeated nine times: "These I give and with these redeem myself and my family." Close behind followed ghosts, who quickly and silently picked up the beans and departed, not to return until the time appointed for the next Lemuria.

Peas

Here are three things to do with lentils or yellow split peas—one each for Thackeray's sailors in "Little Billee." Going to sea with beef, captain's biscuits, and pickled pork, they ate so well that, by the time they crossed the equator, there was nothing left but one split pea.

As to the recipes, which require many times more the one pea in the sailor's ration, the first is hot, the second hotter, and the third mild and gentle and rather sweet.

FAHSOULIA BEYTHA WATEFAH ⌘ 4

This came back from Egypt along with a water buffalo hassock and a pile of floor cushions.

1 *pound lentils or split peas*
3 *large onions, chopped*
3 *tablespoons butter*
¼ *teaspoon turmeric*
¼ *teaspoon pepper*
½ *teaspoon allspice*
1 *teaspoon salt*
1 *large apple, chopped*

Soak the peas overnight, drain, add fresh water, and cook until tender (about 30 minutes to an hour). Drain, but reserve some liquid. Brown the onions in butter, add the seasonings, and stir well. Now dump in the chopped apple and cook and stir until the apple is tender. Mix well with the peas and reheat, adding a little liquid if necessary. Serve with rice as a main dish. This is also a good side dish with lamb, pork, or poultry.

DHALL CURRY ⌘ 4–6

Be sure there are lots of rice and hard rolls or sesame crackers and wine to minimize the effect of being aflame. Or go easy on the cayenne.

½ *pound lentils or split peas*
½ *teaspoon salt*
3 *medium onions, chopped*
2 *green peppers, chopped, seeds removed*
2 *large cloves garlic, chopped*
1 *can green chilies, seeded and chopped*
2 *tablespoons butter*
1 *teaspoon curry powder (more is better, but watch it) cayenne to taste*

Soak the peas overnight, drain, add fresh water and salt, and cook until tender. Drain, but reserve a little liquid. Sauté the vegetables briefly—they should be somewhat crisp. Stir in the curry powder and cayenne and mix everything together well. Simmer about 10 minutes and serve with rice. Fried sausage is good with this.

D. A. R. LENTILS AND HONEY ✌ 4

1 *pound lentils or split peas*
6 *slices uncooked bacon, chopped*
1 *teaspoon salt*
¼ *teaspoon pepper*
1 *teaspoon dry mustard*
¼ *cup chutney*
½ *cup honey*

Soak the peas overnight, drain, add fresh water and salt, and cook until tender. Mix all the ingredients, pour into a covered baking dish and bake 30 minutes in a slow oven—about 325°. Remove the cover and bake 30 minutes longer. Add a little of the reserve liquid if necessary. This smacks of the Middle West and Grant Wood and goes well with brown bread and cole slaw.

Rice

"They had best not stir the rice, though it sticks in the pot," is Cervantes' advice, and it holds true today. Another bit of wisdom is to know which rice is which.

There are, according to those who collect such data, more than fifty varieties of rice. Which may or may not be astounding information when one considers that rice is the major part of the diet for over two-thirds of the world's people.

For Poor Poets four varieties will do: long grain brown and brown pearl, long grain white and white pearl. (White rice is brown rice that has had the outside covering with its vitamin Bs polished away. But some people prefer white and some dishes demand it, so there is little sense involving oneself in a nutritional hassle.)

Brown rice takes longer to cook than white; its texture is pleasantly chewy.

White pearl rice cooks a bit faster; the result is slightly moist, with the grains tending to stick together. This makes it easier to eat with chopsticks. When used in dishes such as Paella and Risotto, more of the sauce is absorbed by the rice, so that it loses its characteristic flavor.

Long grain white rice cooks the fastest and the result is drier, with the grains tending to remain separate.

After much experimentation I have finally settled on the Chinese method of rice cookery. Pour rice into rapidly boiling salted water in a fine stream, so that the water will not stop boiling. Cover loosely, lower the heat, and simmer until tender—about 20 minutes. Plop the rice into a strainer and rinse with hot water, then put it in a pan in a very low oven to keep warm. But don't leave it there long!

Another method—and this is good if the rice is to be held for anywhere up to an hour—is to put a little oil in a pan over high heat. Add the rice and shake the pan until the rice looks a little chalky. Pour in boiling water to cover, put a tight lid on the pan, lower the heat, and simmer until all the water is absorbed and the rice is done. This technique requires a bit of practice, for different rices absorb different amounts of water.

Leftover rice can be refrigerated or frozen and reheated simply by pouring boiling water over it.

What could be a problem often arises after the rice has been cooked: several unexpected and very hungry poets arrive. It must be a universal happening, for almost every area has a solution and every solution a different name. Among them:

PEAS AND RICE

Toss hot cooked peas with twice as much steamed rice, more or less, and a little butter. Stir in a sprinkling of chili teppin, seeded and crushed, to taste. This is especially good with ham or chicken or fried fish.

BEANS AND RICE

Substitute drained canned kidney or red beans for the peas in the above recipe, and omit the chili teppin. Sprinkle with parched sesame seeds.

This combination is a holiday dish in Japan; a sharecropper's dinner in the South; a standby recipe from the nuns of Guadalupe; and, near the Mediterranean, a somewhat color-conscious delight called Moors and Christians. The latter is made with black beans.

HOPPING JOHN

Drop a ham bone into the water in which the rice is cooking, later adding peas or beans as above. If the ham bone hasn't been too well gnawed previously, this makes a good main dish.

PILAF JUSTINE II ・ 4–6

Pre-dinner philosophizing has a way of going on until the jug is empty, or someone is sent out for more, and that is emptied, too. As noted above, rice steamed in the usual manner doesn't sit out this sort of socializing well. Not to say that Pilaf can't be overcooked, but the results aren't so disastrous.

1½ *cups rice (or half rice and half bulgur)*	½ *cup Greek olives*
	2 *tablespoons capers*
1 *tablespoon olive oil*	3 *cups boiling water*

Combine rice, oil, olives, and capers in a casserole. Pour in the boiling water, cover, and bake for 30 minutes at 400°, then turn off the oven, give the rice a stir, and let it sit uncovered for 5 or 10 minutes longer.

RICE AND EGGS

Breakfast? Lunch? Snack? Here is an anytime dish with quantity dependent on appetite (and how much rice is left over).

leftover rice	*salt*
eggs	*crushed chili peppers or*
butter	*chili powder*

Heat the rice. Fry eggs in butter. Turn the rice onto a warmed plate, top with the eggs, a pinch of salt, and crushed chili peppers to taste.

GRANT AVENUE FRIED RICE II   ♋ 4–6

2 *tablespoons peanut oil*
1 *bunch green onions, sliced*
2 *or 3 cups cooked rice*
2 *eggs*
2 *teaspoons soy sauce*
1 *cup diced cooked chicken, ham, or pork*
1 *cup bean sprouts or thinly sliced vegetables*

Sauté the onions in the oil. Gently stir in the rice, and when it is heated, add the eggs that have been beaten with the soy sauce, the chicken, and the sprouts. Turn once or twice until everything is just heated through.

Japanese fried rice is concocted with less onion and, for sure, a handful of chopped raw spinach. But the rice isn't fried. Instead (except for the eggs, which are added just before serving) the whole is simmered gently in chicken or fish stock for 5 minutes.

NASI GORENG   ♋ 4–6

The Dutch East Indies version of fried rice is an elegant dish on a hot day. A fried egg is plunked on top of each serving, with sweet pickles, chutney, and sliced tomato to set it off. Beer is in order.

2 *onions, chopped*
1 *clove garlic, minced*
3 *chili teppins, seeded and chopped*
4 *tablespoons salad oil*
1 *to 2 cups cooked ham, bacon, chicken, or pork, diced*
4 *cups cold cooked rice*

Fry onions, garlic, and peppers slowly in oil until the onion is lightly brown. Add the meat and cook and stir an additional 5 or so minutes. Toss in the rice and mix well, adding a little more oil if necessary. Heat well and serve.

RICE WITH GREEN CHILIES ↻ 6

3 cups cooked rice
2 cups sour cream
½ pound mild Cheddar cheese, diced
1 can green chilies, chopped
    salt

Combine all ingredients, pack in a buttered baking dish, and heat for 30 minutes at 350°.

TURTA ↻ 4–6

4 eggs	1 cup grated mild Cheddar
3 tablespoons olive oil	cheese
2 cups cooked rice	salt and pepper

Beat three of the eggs and then stir in the other ingredients. Pour into a buttered baking dish and top with the remaining beaten egg. Bake 45 minutes at 350°. Serve as is or with any Italian sauce.

RICE PALAESTRA ↻ 4–6

Attributed to the lovely slave who so prettily bent and wriggled her hips while stirring the pot. This is an excellent main dish that also goes well with chicken.

3 tablespoons butter	1½ cups raw rice
1 onion, chopped fine	3 cups chicken stock
1 clove garlic, minced	1½ teaspoons salt
4 lettuce leaves, shredded	pepper
1 small can sliced mush-	1 cup cooked peas
rooms, undrained	1 or 2 pimientos, chopped
1 cup stewed tomatoes	¼ cup raisins, plumped in
4 sausages, diced	hot water

Sauté the onion in butter. Add all but the last three ingredients, mix well, and pour into a casserole with a tight cover. Bake at 400° for a half hour. Toss in the peas, pimiento, and raisins just before serving.

RIJSTAFEL

For the really mad poet, who wants to celebrate in the grand manner, and who has the time, cash, energy, space, dishes—as well as enough hungry friends—the Javanese rijstafel.

It requires mountains of steamed rice and as many condiments and side dishes as can be manufactured, arranged on the table, piled on each plate of rice, and consumed. Fifty-boy rijstafel is considered acceptable in the East Indies, albeit overwhelming for studio entertaining. Ten or so bowls from the following list should be impressive enough. And have the cook in a swivet.

Called for also are beer (preferably dark and plentiful) and an abundance of paper napkins or small towels wrung out in warm water.

1. *Mango chutney*
2. *Grated coconut*
3. *Chopped orange peel*
4. *Chopped grapefruit peel*

5. *Chopped green onions*
6. *Chopped sweet green pepper*
7. *Diced pineapple*
8. *Chopped roasted peanuts*
9. *Raisins, scalded to plump, and drained*
10. *Fried bananas, dusted with brown sugar, cinnamon, and cloves*
11. *Hot pickled peppers*
12. *Watermelon pickles*
13. *Small tomatoes stuffed with cucumbers*
14. *Pickled eggs*
15. *Pickled cucumbers*
16. *Pickled fish*
17. *Meat Sambal: ground meat and liver, garlic, shredded coconut, and Sambal* to taste. Fry slowly and moisten with meat stock.*
18. *Fish Sambal: equal parts of fish and sweet potatoes, both thinly sliced and fried in oil with Sambal to taste*
19. *Fried chicken*
20. *Fried shrimp*
21. *Fried or boiled fish*
22. *Fried eggs with garlic and sliced tomatoes*
23. *Servendel: diced beef or pork mixed with shredded coconut, peanuts, salt, and hot sauce, and fried*
24. *Fish (i.e., codfish) croquettes*
25. *Sajourmenny: any vegetables cut in small strips and simmered in coconut milk, curry powder, garlic, and onion*
26. *Sambal**

Plain steamed rice or rijstafel, not forgetting that Gautama divided all of mankind into ten classifications, with Buddha first, the counterpart of hell tenth—and rice second.

* A recipe for Sambal is on page 168.

Pasta

Pasta ranges in size from hair-thin Oriental noodles to the broad Italian lasagne and fat manicotti. From the poet, who prefers alphabets, to the dreamer, who chooses wheels or stars, there is a multitude of shapes. Add to this the wide range of flavors: spinach, tomato, carrot, onion, herbs and spices, powdered tea, pounded shrimp, eggs.

Poor Poets of the Far East were eating pasta products in 5000 B.C. And today's Poor Poet, if he chose, might spend a lifetime of pasta dinners without ever repeating the same recipe twice. Though he might suffer from obesity.

Here is a handful to start with.

PASTA WITH CHEESE AND CLAMS ⌖ 4

12 *ounces pasta**
4 *slices bacon*
½ *cup butter*
3 *cloves garlic*
1 *6½-ounce can minced clams*
1 *cup grated Parmesan cheese*

While the pasta is cooking to al dente stage, fry the bacon, drain, and crumble. Melt butter and add the garlic, pressed, and the drained clams. Toss this, along with the cheese, into the hot drained pasta, and top with the crumbled bacon.

* Green noodles for eye appeal, shells for a seaside mood, or spaghetti, fettucini, or egg noodles if that's what's on hand. Alphabets simply won't do unless one wishes to eat with a spoon.

NOODLES IN BUTTER ଓ 6

1 *pound egg noodles, cooked*
3 *tablespoons butter*
1 *pound cottage cheese*
1 *egg yolk*
   salt to taste
1 *or 2 tablespoons poppy seed*

Melt butter in a heavy frying pan and sauté cooked noodles until golden brown. This calls for some watching and stirring dexterity, as the noodles should not be allowed to turn into a large pancake. Mix egg yolk and salt with cottage cheese, and pour over the noodles. Allow the mixture to heat throughout. Serve with a generous sprinkling of poppy seeds.

BLUE CHEESE NOODLES ଓ 4

12 *ounces egg noodles*	1 *cup crumbled blue*
$\frac{1}{4}$ *cup butter*	*cheese*
$\frac{1}{2}$ *cup cream or rich milk*	1 *cup shredded mild white cheese*

While noodles are cooking to just tender, melt the butter in a pan and add the cream, cheese, and pepper. When the mixture is heated, toss in the drained noodles and shake the pan a few times. Serve immediately, but certainly not on *white* plates.

NOODLES WITH ALMONDS AND SEEDS ଓ 4–6

This is good as a main dish, or an accompaniment to pot roast. For those who like them, the addition of a handful of raisins is in order.

½ cup shredded almonds
½ pound noodles
4 tablespoons butter
2 tablespoons poppy seed

While the noodles are cooking (about 10 minutes) and draining, brown nuts in butter. Slip noodles into a warm bowl, pour over the butter, nuts, and poppy seed, stir once or twice, and that's it.

If dinner is delayed, the dish can be kept hot over boiling water.

NOODLES WITH HAM AND BUTTERMILK ℭ 4

½ pound noodles
1¼ cups diced ham
1 onion
1 cup buttermilk
2 eggs
1 cup grated Cheddar cheese
1 teaspoon Worcestershire
  salt and pepper to taste

Cook and drain noodles and chop the onion. Combine eggs and Worcestershire with buttermilk. Now, with all ingredients at hand, and a buttered baking dish for a base, begin making layers of noodles, ham, onion, cheese, and buttermilk-egg. Sprinkle intermittently with salt and pepper. When the building process is completed, cover the dish and bake for 30 minutes at 375°. Uncover and bake for an additional 15 minutes.

My great aunt's Cousin Carrie, who passed this recipe on to me, advised using chopped cabbage if there was no ham to be had. She further noted that a combination of chopped apples and raisins was another substitute that she liked a lot.

NOODLES BASILICO

½ pound noodles
2 packages cream cheese or ½ pint cottage cheese
1 small can chopped black olives
4 tablespoons butter
½ teaspoon crushed basil

Put cooked and drained noodles and butter in a low oven or over boiling water while combining the cheese, olives, and basil. Toss everything gently but thoroughly, allow to heat well, and the dish is ready to serve.

PASTA OMELET

A true Poor Poet dish, Pasta Omelet is based on what is on hand at the moment. It is equally good hot or cold and travels well in a camera bag, a paint box, or even a pocket—not a rear pants pocket, though.

olive oil	*diced mozzarella cheese*
garlic	*eggs*
leftover plain pasta	*grated Parmesan cheese*
diced salami	

Heat the oil and garlic in a skillet or omelet pan. Chop the pasta and mix it with the salami and mozzarella. Discard garlic and press the pasta mixture into the pan. Beat enough eggs with Parmesan and a little water to seep around the pasta and hold it together. Brown slowly on one side, turn, and brown on the other.

Pasta Omelet can be made with leftover spaghetti that has been bathed in sauce. It can be more omelet than pasta or vice versa.

MR. MUSCETTI'S TURKEY DRESSING

Sufficient to stuff a 20-pound turkey, this dressing may also be used to fill manicotti, layer with lasagne, or (and this was the original intention) make real homemade ravioli.

1 *beef brain, parboiled and chopped*
1 *pound ground veal*
1 *pound ground pork*
  olive oil
2 *pounds spinach or Swiss chard, parboiled and chopped*
3 *cloves garlic, chopped*
3 *stalks celery, chopped*
1 *medium onion, chopped*
2 *tablespoons chopped parsley*
$\frac{1}{8}$ *teaspoon each ground allspice, cloves, cinnamon, and poultry seasoning*
5 *eggs*
1 *cup grated Parmesan cheese*
$\frac{1}{2}$ *cup grated bread*
  salt and pepper to taste

Heat a little olive oil in a large frying pan and brown veal and pork lightly. Blend in spinach, garlic, celery, parsley, and onion. Add the chopped brain and spices, and cook for several minutes. Turn the mixture into a large bowl and allow to cool slightly. Then, using a big wooden spoon, beat in the eggs, one at a time. Toss in cheese and bread, and beat a little more. If the mixture seems too dry, another egg or two will remedy the matter, and the stuffing is ready to be used as desired.

SPAGHETTI SAUCE   ᘓ 6–8

Start this spaghetti sauce at the break of a cold and dreary day. (In northern latitudes, arise an hour earlier.) Simmer it on and off as the weather continues or worsens. Stir and taste occasionally, adding more wine if the sauce becomes too thick. And, in the evening, with a blustery wind invading any crack, serve it over a platter of steaming spaghetti.

3 or 4 *large cloves garlic*	1 *can tomato paste*
2 *medium onions*	¼ *teaspoon sugar*
4 *tablespoons olive oil*	1 *teaspoon salt*
1 *pound lean ground beef*	¼ *teaspoon cayenne*
½ *cup chopped celery*	1 *teaspoon each rosemary,*
1 *cup dry red wine*	*basil, thyme, and*
1 *large can solid pack tomatoes*	*oregano*

Chop garlic and onions and sauté in oil until golden. Add ground beef and cook and stir with a fork until meat is brown. Drop in all other ingredients, in any order; lower heat; cover and simmer for several hours, at least, or preferably as noted above.

ABSENT-MINDED POET'S   ↄ 4
SPAGHETTI SAUCE

This sauce can be made on the spur of the moment and is enough for a pound of spaghetti.

¼ *pound bacon or salt pork*	1 *or 2 teaspoons coarse*
¼ *cup olive oil*	*ground pepper*
1 *clove garlic, crushed*	¼ *cup grated Romano cheese*

Dice the bacon or salt pork and sauté it, with the garlic, in the olive oil until nearly crisp. Pour over hot spaghetti, add the pepper, and toss. Sprinkle with cheese.

A quite different flavor is achieved if two beaten eggs are tossed with the hot spaghetti just before the bacon-oil sauce is added.

ONE POTS

The fine One Pot has innumerable advantages inherent in its name: the dishwasher, who often doubles as cook, is saved for future culinary orgies; the necessity of purchasing an extra dish for serving is eliminated; the dish itself is easy on both the budget and chef; and, a One Pot may be carried to the home of an ailing friend, to the park, or to a church social.

Except for an occasional stir and taste during cooking, the One Pot requires little attention. However, there *are* two rules: never use weary vegetables; never allow the contents to boil.

One Pots That Require No Meat

The stability of produce prices is comparable to that of an artistic temperament. Thus, the dishes that appear first on the assumption that they are least extravagant might—during a period of inclement weather and bad crops—prove to be exorbitant. Then again, all ingredients for the last dish might just be discovered the day the refrigerator is defrosted: bonus dinner.

But here's one relatively unaffected by defrosting or season, though it tastes best on a cold night.

A RAGOUT OF ONIONS ℞ 2

4 *large onions*
4 *tablespoons butter*
½ *cup gravy or bouillon*
¼ *teaspoon dry mustard*
   salt and pepper to taste

Peel and slice onions, separating rings. Cook in butter, stirring to prevent sticking. When the onions are soft and golden add the gravy into which the mustard has been blended. Season with salt and pepper and stir gently until the ragout is thick. Serve to two along with thick slabs of dark rye bread and butter, a green salad, and red wine.

ELK RIVER STEW ℞ 4–6

6 *potatoes*   ½ *cup milk*
1 *large onion*   *salt and pepper*
2 *tablespoons butter* 6 *pilot crackers*
½ *cup cream*

Slice the potatoes and onion and cook together in water to cover. When the vegetables are done stir in the butter, cream, milk, and seasonings. Serve with pilot crackers and a vegetable salad.

POTATO DEUTSCHER ℞ 6

7 *potatoes*   *pepper*
6 *slices stale bread* 2 *cups milk*
2 *eggs*   1 *cup sour cream*
1 *teaspoon salt*

Grate the potatoes, rinse in cold water, and press dry. Soak bread in milk, beat in eggs and seasonings, and then stir in the potatoes. Pour into a buttered dish, top with sour cream, and bake at 350° for 45 minutes.

ZUCCHINI WITH ALMONDS   ℭ 4–6

1 *tablespoon each butter and olive oil*
1½ *pounds zucchini, sliced*
⅓ *cup chopped green onion*
¼ *teaspoon each basil, oregano, and garlic salt*
1 *small tomato, diced*
1 *tablespoon flour*
1 *cup grated Parmesan cheese*
⅔ *cup chopped roasted almonds*
pepper

Build this dish in an earthenware casserole that has lost its cover.

Sauté the zucchini, onion, and seasonings in butter and olive oil for 4 or 5 minutes. Stir in the tomato, a sprinkling of flour, and half the cheese and almonds. Strew the remaining cheese and almonds over the top. Bake for 30 minutes at 350°.

Somehow, a green salad that contains sliced hard-cooked eggs is just right with this. And—don't forget the roll and butter.

PETER'S PEPPER STEW   ℭ 4

3 *large onions*
1 *clove garlic*
4 *tablespoons olive oil*
5 *large green peppers*
2 *green chili peppers*
3 *or 4 tomatoes*
3 *large potatoes*
1 *teaspoon marjoram leaves*
salt and pepper

Sauté the onion, cut into large chunks, and the minced garlic in olive oil until they are limp and golden. Cut the vegetables in generous pieces, being sure to omit any trace of pepper seeds, which can prove unbearably hot. Now add the vegetables to the pot, along with the seasonings, cover, and cook 45 minutes, or until the potatoes are tender. Check intermittently to see that the pot does not become too dry, and stir with caution. Serve the stew in earthenware bowls and accompanied by crusty bread and butter.

RED CABBAGE WITH WINE   ↻ 2–4

This dish, along with mashed potatoes or potato pancakes, makes a good cold night dinner. One or two bouillon cubes dissolved in the hot water make for a richer dish.

1 *head red cabbage*
red wine vinegar
1 *tablespoon butter or bacon fat*
1 *tablespoon brown sugar*
1 *teaspoon salt*
pepper to taste and a dash of nutmeg
1 *onion, finely chopped*
1 *or 2 apples, finely chopped*
1 *tablespoon vinegar*
1 *cup red wine*
cloves or caraway seeds (optional)
¼ *cup currant jelly*

Slice the cabbage and soak in red wine vinegar mixed with equal parts of water for 30 minutes. Melt the butter in a saucepan and add the drained cabbage along with the sugar, salt, pepper, nutmeg, and onion. Cover and simmer for 20 minutes or until the cabbage begins to appear a little dry, lifting the lid every so often to stir. Add one cup hot water, the red wine, vinegar, and chopped apple. A few cloves or caraway seeds may be tossed in now. Cover and let cook slowly until tender—about 25 minutes. Just before serving stir in the currant jelly.

MATTER-PANEER ↻ 4

1 *onion, sliced thin*
2 *tablespoons butter*
1 *10-ounce package frozen peas*
1 *teaspoon salt*
¾ *teaspoon curry powder*
¾ *teaspoon turmeric*
2 *mint leaves (if possible)*
1 *pint large curd cottage cheese, well drained*
¼ *teaspoon chili powder*

Sauté the onions in butter until soft. Blend in the curry powder and turmeric. Add the peas, salt, and mint leaves. Cover and cook 5 to 8 minutes, or until the peas are just tender. Just before serving blend in the cottage cheese and chili powder. Let stand a few minutes to heat through, but don't continue cooking or the cottage cheese will melt.

Sliced tomatoes with cracked pepper, and corn or sesame seed crackers go with this.

CORN PUDDING ↻ 6

Just (almost, anyway) like mother used to make.

1 *one-pound can cream-style corn*
1 *to 1½ cups any or all of the following: diced celery, chopped ripe olives, onions, pimiento, or green pepper*
1 *tablespoon butter*
2 *eggs*
1 *teaspoon salt*
¼ *teaspoon each pepper and dry mustard*
½ *teaspoon paprika or chili powder*
½ *cup cracker crumbs, crushed cornflakes, or grated Parmesan cheese*

Melt the butter in an earthenware pot and simmer the mixed vegetables (except the corn) gently. Beat eggs slightly and add to the pot along with the corn and seasonings. Mix well. Sprinkle crumbs or cheese over the top and bake for 45 minutes at 350°.

NACHOS ⁂ 4

Memories of weekly forays to a then-dusty border town for guitar lessons and a supper of tequila and *nachos*. Today a more sober poet accompanies *nachos* with green salad and, perhaps, a bowl of black beans.

12 *corn tortillas*	1 *4-ounce can chopped*
1 *pound Jack cheese*	*green chilies*
	butter or oil

Lightly butter or oil a skillet or baking pan. Cut the cheese into twelve pieces. Roll a piece of cheese and a bit of chili in each tortilla and place in a lightly buttered or oiled skillet or baking pan. Be sure that the tortilla edges are down; otherwise the *nachos* will fly open and not deserve their name: "flat noses." Now either heat the dish on top of the stove or in a 350° oven, just until the cheese melts.

A PORTUGUESE PANCAKE ⁂ 6

2 *pounds zucchini squash*
1 *large onion*
1 *green pepper*
1 *or 2 cloves garlic*
2 *or 3 sprigs each parsley and celery tops*
5 *tablespoons olive oil*
1 *8-ounce tin tomato sauce or 2 large tomatoes*
1 *teaspoon each basil and oregano*
5 *eggs*
½ *cup milk*
½ *cup grated cheese*
   salt, pepper, and paprika

Use a heavy frying pan with a lid. Dice the vegetables and brown quickly in the olive oil. Add tomato sauce or tomatoes, basil, and oregano and simmer until the mixture is barely moist. Beat eggs with milk and a little salt and pepper, and pour over the vegetables. Cover and cook until the eggs begin to set. Sprinkle with cheese and paprika and brown under the broiler. Serve in pie-shaped wedges.

One Pots with Meat

JAGER KOHL ↻ 4

½ *pound bacon or sausages*
2 *or* 3 *large potatoes*
1 *small head cabbage*
2 *tablespoons flour*
   salt, cracked pepper, and cider vinegar to taste
½ *pint sour cream or yogurt*

Fry the bacon in a frying pan with lid. Drain off most of the fat and add thick slices of peeled potatoes and cabbage. Sprinkle flour over the vegetables, add water to barely cover, along with salt and a dash of vinegar. Cover and cook slowly 45 minutes to an hour. Serve along with a bowl of sour cream, cracked pepper, and a little cruet of vinegar for those who like a sharper flavor. Rye bread and butter and a salad of apples and raisins rounds out this meal.

LOUISE'S DUTCH DISH

"Potatoes is the best vegetable," declares a very young friend. And here is another One Pot based on that "best vegetable."

To figure out how much of what to use, multiply the

following ingredients by the number of persons sitting hungrily by. An ample Dutch Dish for one requires:

1 *each small onion, apple, and potato*
2 *or* 3 *slices bacon*
pepper

Fry the bacon, but do not allow it to get crisp. In the meantime, peel and grate the vegetables and apple. Break up the bacon, drain off a little fat, add the vegetables, and fry gently until everything is done. Turn out on a hot plate and grind lots of pepper over the top. Eat as is or with fried eggs . . . and hot, strong coffee.

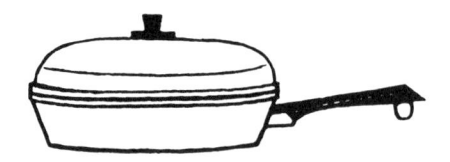

HOG AND HOMINY ॡ 2–3

$\frac{3}{4}$ *pound bacon, ham, or sausages*
2 *tablespoons butter*
1 *#2$\frac{1}{2}$ can hominy*
$\frac{1}{2}$ *cup milk*
1 *teaspoon paprika*
$\frac{1}{4}$ *teaspoon salt*

Use a frying pan with lid. Cut up the meat and sauté in butter. Move the meat to the center of the pan, pour drained hominy around, sprinkle with paprika and salt, and add the milk. Cover and simmer 5 or 10 minutes, or until all the milk is absorbed.

Hog and Hominy presents possibilities. Green onions can be sautéed with the meat. Chili powder can replace the paprika. Or the milk can be increased to a cup or more, and a teaspoon of gumbo filé powder mixed in just before serving. In this case bowls, not plates, for eating. Furthermore, the name can be changed to protect the delicate.

POCKET-POOR ~ 4

2½ *pounds sweet onions*
1½ *pounds potatoes*
¾ *cup rice*
½ *pound smoked sausages*
  salt, cracked pepper, and cider vinegar to taste

Peel potatoes, slice thick, and bring to a boil in water just to cover. Add the onions, which are also in thick slices, rice, and cut-up sausages. Season with a little salt, cover, and simmer slowly for about 30 minutes. Just before serving sprinkle a little cider vinegar and freshly cracked pepper over the dish. A vegetable salad with a mild sour cream or yogurt dressing goes well, as does rye or pumpernickel bread with lots of butter.

TIN CAN SPECIAL ~ 4

Even the poet with such limited equipment as a frying pan, knife, and spoon can put together this dish.

2 *medium onions*
  butter
1 *#2 can corned beef hash*
1 *#2 can baked beans*
1 *#2 can tomatoes, drained*
4 *eggs*

Slice the onions and sauté them in butter until golden. Empty the tins into the frying pan and stir well. Put the pan into a 375° oven and bake until brown. Break the eggs on top of the hash and return to oven until done.

PEASANT POTATOES ↻ 6–8

 6 *boiled potatoes*
 3 *hard-cooked eggs*
 1 *teaspoon salt*
 1 *cup sour cream*
 1 *cup diced ham or smoked sausage*
 ½ *cup bread crumbs*
 2 *tablespoons melted butter*
 ½ *cup heavy cream*

Slice the potatoes and eggs and combine in a buttered baking dish with the salt, sour cream, and ham. Pour cream over the top and sprinkle with the crumbs that have been mixed with butter. Bake 30 minutes at 450°.

POTATO SALAD—OVEN METHOD II ↻ 6

Back again is the "best vegetable," found now in a dish that is just fine for a rained-out picnic.

6 *cooked potatoes*	2 *tablespoons vinegar*
4 *slices bacon*	*salt and pepper*
1 *onion*	

Peel and slice the potatoes into a shallow baking dish. Dice the bacon, slice the onion, and cook them together until the bacon is crisp. Add the vinegar, bring to a boil, and pour over the potatoes. Season, cover, and let stand in a 300° oven until warm.

For a change, Oven Potato Salad II can be sprinkled with chopped fresh parsley or dill or both just before serving.

SAUSAGES WITH YAMS AND APPLES ♋ 6

Designed for the first crisp autumn day.

2 *large yams or sweet potatoes*
3 *large cooking apples*
1 *pound bulk or link pork sausage*
⅔ *cup brown sugar*
½ *teaspoon salt*

Boil, peel, and slice the yams and core and slice the apples. If using bulk sausage, make 6 patties. Brown sausage in skillet and set aside. Drain most of the fat from the pan and then lay in it alternate layers of yams and apples. Sprinkle each layer with brown sugar and salt. Top with the sausage, cover, and bake 30 minutes at 350°. Remove the cover and bake until the apples are soft.

Cole slaw is a good companion. So is cranberry sauce. And so, too, hot corn bread with lots of butter.

GREEN PEA PIE ♋ 6

1 *9-inch unbaked pastry shell*
8 *slices bacon*
2 *medium onions*
1 *10-ounce package frozen peas, partially defrosted*
4 *eggs*
1½ *cups milk*
1 *teaspoon salt*
¼ *teaspoon hickory smoked salt*
⅛ *teaspoon pepper*

Dice, fry, and drain the bacon. Pour off all but about ¼ cup drippings and in this sauté the thinly sliced onions until limp. Layer onions, bacon, and peas in pastry shell.

Beat the other ingredients and pour over. Bake in the lower part of a 400° oven for 40 to 45 minutes, or until the custard is set.

10-MINUTE HAM AND GREEN BEANS   ℧ 4–6

This is really a two-pot, but because it's so speedy to put together it's been sneaked into the One Pot category.

2 *cups cooked cubed ham*	1 *tablespoon butter*
1 *tablespoon drippings*	1 *tablespoon flour*
1 10-*ounce package frozen green beans, cooked tender-crisp*	½ *cup milk*
	½ *cup sour cream*
	1 *tablespoon soy sauce*
1 4-*ounce can water chestnuts*	⅓ *cup cracker crumbs*
	4 *tablespoons melted butter*

Haul out the frying pan that can double as baking and serving dish. In it brown the ham and pour off any drippings before adding the green beans and water chestnuts, drained and thinly sliced. Leave pan over low heat. In pot number two melt 1 tablespoon butter. Stir in the flour and add the milk. Cook, stirring constantly, until mixture thickens. Add the sour cream and soy sauce, mix well, and then pour over ham and vegetables. Sprinkle crumbs and melted butter over all. Place the dish under the broiler for 2 or 3 minutes, or until the crumbs are lightly browned.

SAFARI SQUASH   ℧ 4

2 *small acorn squash or*	1 *chili teppin*
1 *small pumpkin*	1 *teaspoon curry powder*
1½ *cups bouillon*	½ *cup yogurt*
½ *pound lean ground beef*	1 *bay leaf*
1 *cup rice*	½ *teaspoon ground cloves*
2 *tablespoons butter*	

Steam the squash for about 20 minutes, or until just tender. Cool, cut in half lengthwise, and scoop out the seeds. (If a pumpkin is used, steam, cook, but leave whole, merely scooping seeds out from the top jack-o-lantern style.) In the meantime cook the beef in the bouillon and drain, reserving the stock. Brown the rice in butter. Add a little salt, the crumbled chili teppin, and one cup of stock. Simmer, covered, until rice is done. Add curry powder, yogurt, and ground beef and stuff the squash with this mixture. Bake for an hour at 350°, basting occasionally with the remaining stock to which the crushed bay leaf and cloves have been added.

SWEET-SOUR PORK ℃ 4

1 *pound lean pork shoulder or leftover pork roast*
fat or oil
1 *cup bouillon*
3 *teaspoons soy sauce*
pepper to taste
2 *large green peppers*
1 *medium onion*
4 *slices pineapple (or equivalent chunk-style)*
3 *tablespoons cornstarch*
$\frac{1}{4}$ *cup cider vinegar*
$\frac{1}{4}$ *cup sugar*
$\frac{1}{2}$ *cup pineapple syrup*

Cut the pork in $\frac{1}{2}$-inch cubes and thoroughly brown in a little fat. Sprinkle with 1 teaspoon soy sauce and a little pepper, pour on the bouillon, and cook very gently, covered, for 20 minutes. (If leftover pork roast is used, heat only to bring the bouillon to a boil.) Cut the green peppers and onions in wedges, add, along with the pineapple pieces, and allow to cook uncovered for 5 minutes. In the meantime, blend the cornstarch, sugar, vinegar, 2 teaspoons soy sauce, and syrup, and add to the above. Cook no longer than 5 additional minutes, stirring all the time. Remember that the vegetables must remain crisp. Serve with steamed rice.

PACIFIC PORK AND CABBAGE ↻ 4

1 *pound lean pork shoulder*
fat or oil
1 *cup diced onion*
1½ *pounds cabbage*
4 *teaspoons soy sauce*
salt and pepper to taste

Cut the pork in thin strips and brown in a little fat. Pile in the onions and shredded cabbage. Stir over high heat for 3 to 5 minutes. Add soy sauce and a little salt and pepper. Cover and continue to cook for 1 or 2 minutes—the vegetables *must* remain crisp. Serve over hot noodles, and additional soy sauce on the side.

CARBONADO ↻ 4–6

2 *large onions*
2 *tablespoons fat*
1 *pound ground beef*
1 *large tomato*
½ *cup bouillon*
3 *large potatoes*
3 *or 4 apples or firm*
  peaches
½ *cup raisins*
salt and pepper

Chop onions and sauté until golden. Add the meat and allow to brown. Stir and crumble the meat with a fork while the browning is progressing. Now add the peeled and cut-up tomato along with the bouillon. Cover and cook slowly 15 minutes. During this interval peel the potatoes and apples and slice them very thin. Now lay them on top of the meat, season with a little salt and pepper, and replace the lid. Simmer until the potatoes are done. Add the raisins about 5 minutes before removing from the fire. It's not at all a bad idea to check every so often, for if it's allowed to dry there is a serious shrinkage problem.

RATATOUILLE, NON-CLASSICAL STYLE ↺ 4

1 *medium eggplant*
2 *onions*
1 *can stewed tomatoes*
1 *bay leaf*
½ *teaspoon brown sugar*
½ *pound lean ground beef*
   olive oil
   salt and pepper

Soak peeled and diced eggplant in salt water for an hour. Then boil until tender with the onions, chopped, crushed bay leaf, and a little salt and pepper. Brown the meat in olive oil and then add to the eggplant-onion mixture along with the stewed tomatoes and brown sugar. Heat well, or better yet, refrigerate overnight, then heat and serve with steamed rice and a dish of cold yogurt.

END-OF-MONTH STROGANOFF ↺ 4

4 *ounces noodles*
¾ *cup sliced onions*
1 *pound ground beef*
   fat or oil
¼ *cup flour*
¾ *teaspoon salt*
   dash pepper
¼ *cup tomato sauce or catsup*
1 *teaspoon Worcestershire*
1 *bouillon cube*
1 *8-ounce can mushroom pieces, with liquid*
1⅓ *cups buttermilk*

Cook noodles and drain. Meanwhile brown the onions and ground beef in a little fat. Remove from the fire and blend in the flour, salt, and pepper. Crumble the bouillon cube and add, along with all other ingredients, and mix everything well. Now stir in the noodles, turn the mixture into a buttered baking dish, and bake for 25 to 30 minutes at 350°.

E-O-M Stroganoff is obviously portable, making it fine for picnics in the back yard or longer pilgrimages. Purists, however, might prefer to serve the stroganoff over the noodles (or rice) and skip the business about the oven.

FRAN'S STUFFED CABBAGE ↺ 6

A One Pot in three parts, Fran's recipe is not at all as complicated as it might first appear.

BASICS

| 1 *medium onion* | 12 *cabbage leaves* |

STUFFING

| $1\frac{1}{2}$ *pounds ground chuck* | $\frac{1}{3}$ *cup chopped parsley* |
| 2 *eggs* | *salt and pepper* |

SAUCE

1 12-*ounce can stewed tomatoes*	2 *tablespoons lemon juice*
1 *cup tomato juice or purée*	3 *tablespoons sugar*
	3 *bay leaves*
6 *to* 8 *ginger snaps*	10 *whole peppercorns*
	1 *teaspoon salt*

Chop the onion and sprinkle it into a shallow baking pan. Steam the cabbage leaves. Mix the filling and divide it among the cabbage leaves. Roll them neatly and place them in *one* layer on the onions. Simmer the sauce for about 5 minutes and pour over the cabbage rolls. Cover and bake 1 hour at 325°. Remove cover and bake an additional 15 minutes.

UP-COUNTRY MEAT BALLS AND VEGETABLES   4–6

What, meat balls again? And why not. The puppy has been put on a hamburger diet, and it is both convenient and permissible to rob from his supply.

2 pounds ground beef
1 egg
1½ teaspoons salt
¼ teaspoon pepper
   dash Worcestershire
½ cup dry red wine or
   water
2 cans beef gravy (or one can gravy and one can red wine)
½ teaspoon marjoram
8 each small carrots, small white onions, small potatoes
   fat or oil
3 or 4 big fresh mushrooms
1 tablespoon butter
   chopped parsley

Mix the first 8 ingredients, make eight or so generous meat balls, and brown in hot fat. Remove to a baking dish. Peel vegetables, leave whole, and cook for about 15 minutes in boiling salted water, then add them to the meat balls. Add gravy and marjoram to the pan in which the meat balls cooked, bring to a boil, and pour over the meat and vegetables. Cover and bake 1 hour at 350°.

When ready to serve, arrange mushroom slices that have been browned in butter, and the chopped parsley, over the dish.

MEATS

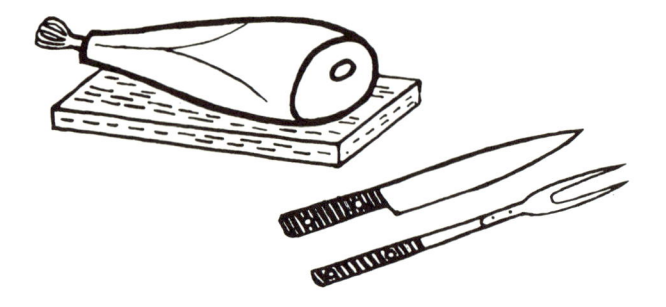

Poor Poets, unless they truly are vegetarians, need meat. It is all well and good to claim that 10 slices of fortified bread will give one the same energy value as a pound of lean beef, or that there are as many calories in three martinis, including the olive, as there are in a fine fillet. Or is it?

Poor Poets need meat because it is better for them than suppers of fortified bread and martinis. They need meat because it is good for them to say, "I had steak for dinner last night," and mean it because it is true.

There are skills to eating meat every (or almost every) night and still maintaining a handful of spare change. And the main one is to let the "weekend specials," not the palate, be the deciding factor in what to eat when. Also important is possession of a good sharp knife and the ability to use it. This latter comes with lots of initial nerve and continued practice. For those weekend specials usually come as is, and any custom cutting required of the butcher will considerably inflate the cost. A good boning knife is really a must, and it's worth one's while to prowl the used hardware stores for one.

There is, nonetheless, the fable of the Poor Poet who spent so much on cutlery that he was condemned to an extended diet of day-old bread and the like.

Heed the message.

Beef

Start with a functional blade chuck roast. Which means four distinct and different meat meals, *not* an enormous Sunday pot roast followed by a week of warmed-overs.

Using the best knife the budget will allow, cut away the strip of meat next to the blade and including the surface on which the grade is stamped. Roll this, with the surface side out, tie with stout string, and there is meal number one: rolled roast.

Next, work on the opposite side, removing the bony edge (but leaving some meat). This is the second meal, which might be a stew or a thick soup.

Exposed now is an oval boneless area. Cut or pull this away and slice for steaks. The flavor is as good as that of the most expensive, and tenderness is guaranteed if a sprinkling of tenderizer is used just before cooking. Another good tenderizing technique is to poke holes in the meat and then give it a generous olive oil bath. And there are others: lemon juice, red wine, beer.

On to meal number four, which now remains on the cutting board: pot roast.

POT ROAST WITH HONEY AND LEMON ↵ 4

Here's a pot roast method that results in good sandwiches if the initial dish is served to two instead of the four indicated.

2 pounds beef cut for pot roast
1 teaspoon garlic salt
1 teaspoon paprika
1 or 2 tablespoons flour
1 or 2 tablespoons shortening
1 tablespoon lemon juice and a slice of rind
1 tablespoon honey
1 bouillon cube
½ cup water
1 small onion, chopped

Rub the beef with salt, paprika, and flour and brown well in hot shortening. Add the remaining ingredients, cover, and let simmer until meat is tender. This will take almost 2 hours. The meat saved for sandwiches should be allowed to cool in the liquid unless the latter has been all used up for gravy.

POT ROAST IN PALANQUIN ℧ 4

2 pounds beef cut for pot roast
½ package dehydrated onion soup mix
½ cup red wine
heavy aluminum foil

Here the aluminum palanquin seals in all the juices and flavor and makes a fine substitute Dutch oven.

Place the beef on a generous piece of foil, sprinkle with onion soup mix, turn up the edges of the foil a bit, and add the wine. Now wrap the meat securely but not too tightly. Lay the palanquin on a baking pan or additional sheet of foil. Bake at 350° for 2 hours. This is good with mashed potatoes, for there is lots of rich brown juice.

POT ROAST WITH CRUMBS ℧ 4 or 5

This is pretty close to a One Pot for the end result is a pot roast surrounded by a rich bread pudding laced with wine and vegetables.

2 to 2½ pounds beef cut for pot roast
1 clove garlic, mashed
1 cup dry bread crumbs
¾ pound carrots, sliced
¼ pound mushrooms, sliced
¼ cup sliced green olives
½ sweet red pepper, diced
1 fresh pig's foot
2 cups dry red table wine
a bouquet garni of parsley, bay, and thyme

Sear the meat in a little fat and sprinkle it with garlic. Surround with the other ingredients, topping with the pig's foot and bouquet garni. Cover the pot tightly, preferably sealing the lid with flour-water paste. Simmer slowly for 2 to 2½ hours, or cook for the same amount of time in a 350° oven.

GARLIC ROLLED ROAST 4

2 pounds beef cut for rolling
2 or 3 cloves of garlic, mashed
olive oil and red wine vinegar

Before rolling the roast, rub with olive oil and a very little red wine vinegar. Then spread with mashed garlic. Roll, tie, and wrap in waxed paper, and allow to stand for several hours.

Brown the roast (remove the paper first, please) in a 500° oven for about 20 minutes. Then lower heat to 300° and continue cooking, allowing 25 to 40 minutes per pound.

ROLLED ROAST, SAUERBRATEN STYLE

✣ 4

>2 pounds beef, cut for rolling
>4 tablespoons dry red wine
>2 tablespoons tarragon vinegar
>½ teaspoon salt
>½ teaspoon pepper
>dash each thyme, mace, sage, allspice, mustard, and cloves
>½ bay leaf, crushed
>1 small onion
>1 small carrot
>sprig of celery

Chop vegetables and combine all ingredients. Then generously slather this mixture over the meat. Roll, with the fat side out, and tie. Wrap the roast in waxed paper and allow it to stand for several hours at room temperature, or overnight in the refrigerator. The longer it stands, up to a point that is, the more distinct will be the sauerbraten flavor.

Roast as in preceding recipe. Potato pancakes go with this.

ROLLED ROAST DAUPHINE

✣ 4

>2 to 2½ pounds rolled roast
>1 or 2 tablespoons shortening
>½ cup each sliced carrots and onions
>½ teaspoon each thyme and marjoram leaves
>½ bay leaf, crushed
>2 big tablespoons chopped parsley
>4 or 5 peppercorns
>1½ cups dry red wine
>¾ cup Madeira wine
>1 cup reconstituted chicken or veal gravy mix

Dry the meat well with paper towels and sear in very hot fat along with the chopped vegetables and herbs. Lower the heat slightly and slosh the red wine over the meat, allowing the juices to become syrupy. Now pour over the Madeira and gravy and allow to come to a boil on top of the stove. Next put the roast into a 250° oven and cook for a half to three-quarters of an hour, basting frequently.

The center cut of the chuck roast, usually reserved for steaks, can also be treated in this manner. In which case the dish becomes Beef Dauphine.

The building of a good stew is to be reserved for a cold day. Dishes in this genre usually improve themselves by sitting on the back of the stove for many hours. Then, just before serving they are brought to a steaming bubbliness.

Avoid the insidious grey-beige stew: thoroughly dry each piece of meat with paper toweling; brown the meat in very hot fat, and don't crowd it in the pan. A task that can prove hot and smoky but one that guarantees a rich brown triumph.

PAPRIKA BEEF ‧ 6

2 *pounds beef cut for stew*	1 *teaspoon salt*
1 *tablespoon oil*	4 *tablespoons paprika*
1 *pound onions*	1 *teaspoon wine vinegar*
1 *teaspoon caraway seeds*	1 *cup dry red wine*
½ *teaspoon marjoram*	

Brown the meat well and set aside. In the meantime, slice onions as thin as possible and sauté until golden. Add caraway seeds, marjoram, salt, and paprika. Stir well and moisten with vinegar. Now return the meat to the pan, add wine, cover tightly, and simmer for about 2 hours. If the dish tends to get too dry, add a little water from time to time. Serve Paprika Beef with buttered noodles. A salad that includes beets and a few tarragon leaves is good to round out the dinner.

STELLA'S BEEF WITH PICKLED ONIONS ℘ 4–6

2 pounds beef cut for stew
1 tablespoon oil
2 one-pound cans stewed tomatoes
4 peppercorns
2 whole cardamom seeds or 1 bay leaf
½ cup pickled onions, with juice
salt to taste

Brown the beef and add peppercorns, cardamom seeds, salt, and stewed tomatoes. Cover and simmer about 2 hours, or until the meat is tender. Pour in the onions and search for the peppercorns and cardamom seeds. Remove these. This stew definitely calls for mashed potatoes.

BEEF STEW WITH WATER CHESTNUTS ℘ 4

¼ pound salt pork
1½ pounds beef cut for stew
1 large clove garlic
1 large onion
1 cup bouillon
1 can tomato sauce
1 tablespoon pickling spices
6 peppercorns
3 potatoes
1 small can water chestnuts
½ teaspoon salt

Dice the salt pork and brown in a heavy pan. Next brown the stew meat, and then the garlic and onion that has been sliced thin. Move this to a baking dish along with the bouillon, tomato sauce, and spices tied in cheesecloth. Cover and bake 1½ hours at 350°. Now add the potatoes, peeled and sliced, and the water chestnuts, drained and sliced thin. Sprinkle with salt. Re-cover and bake an additional 45 minutes.

BEEF IN RUM   ↄ 4–6

A celebration feast for the not-so-Poor Poet, who must not shirk on any of the ingredients.

2 *pounds beef cut for stew*	1 *tablespoon wine vinegar*
¼ *cup Jamaica rum*	1 *bay leaf*
2 *tablespoons butter*	2 *cups water*
2 *tablespoons flour*	2 *cups sliced fresh mushrooms*
1 *teaspoon salt*	
1 *tablespoon catsup*	½ *cup chopped parsley*
1 *tablespoon currant jelly*	

Sprinkle half the rum over the meat and let stand for several hours (overnight is better). Brown the meat in the butter and remove to a baking dish that later will be used for serving. Blend and brown the flour in the butter remaining in the pan. Stir in the salt, catsup, jelly, vinegar, bay leaf, water, and the remaining rum. Pour this, along with half the mushrooms, over the meat. Cover and bake at 350° for 1½ hours. Now arrange the rest of the mushrooms over the meat, re-cover, and allow to bake another 20 to 30 minutes. Serve with a mound of parsley piled in the center of the dish, and a big bowl of steamed rice or mashed potatoes on the side.

Lamb

An awesome spectacle to the Poor Poet is the sign, "Leg of Lamb—SPECIAL." Shall he splurge—roast the whole thing—invite all hungry friends—have a true feast? Or shall he turn away from this temptation, which could likewise turn out to be an extravagant gesture?

The best alternative is advanced practice with home butchering, although a leg of lamb is a bit more tricky than attacking a chuck or veal roast.

Although it requires a small saw, the easiest method is to slice several steaks from the sirloin end, leaving the balance for a roast.

Somewhat more involved, for only a boning knife is used, is to cut into the meat along the pelvic bone until the ball and socket bone are reached. The leg is then cut from the opposite side straight to the socket-bone cut. This results in a solid piece of meat for stew or curry, bones for soup, and the remainder of the leg for a roast. For Poor Poets who find the sight of the round socket bone protruding slightly from the roast unaesthetic, use of a saw or individual décor is recommended.

NOMADIC LAMB ៷ 8

Follow the lead of the nomads—invite seven Poor Poets to gather together around the barbecue or fireplace.

2 *pounds lamb (sliced, cubed, or even chops)*
1 *cup soy sauce*
½ *cup sherry*
1½ *teaspoons sesame oil*
¼ *teaspoon MSG*
¼ *teaspoon pepper*
1 *clove garlic, crushed*
3 *green onions, chopped*

Combine all ingredients and marinate all day, or at least for several hours. Shake the marinade from the meat. Broil the pieces on a greased grill until tender. Serve Nomadic Lamb with rice or with heated flour tortillas.

LAMB SHANKS WITH OKRA ♋ 4

4 *lamb shanks*
2 *tablespoons oil*
½ *cup chopped onion*
1 *one-pound can tomatoes*
1 *teaspoon salt*
¼ *teaspoon each pepper, sage, basil, thyme*
thick slice of lemon
1 *can baby okra*

Heat oil in a heavy skillet and brown the lamb shanks. Reduce the heat, add the onion, and sauté until tender. Drain any excess fat and stir in everything except the okra. Cover and simmer 45 minutes or until the meat is tender. Add the okra during the last 10 minutes of cooking time.

GROUNDNUT CHOP II ♋ 4–6

Poets and philosophers of ancient China are said to have named jellied lamb accompanied by fragrant wine their favorite repast. Today's Poor Poet can, of course, build an aspic around leftover lamb—or prepare the following.

2 *pounds diced cooked lamb*
2 *tablespoons olive oil*
2¾ *cups water*
1 *teaspoon paprika*
⅔ *cup crunchy peanut butter*
¼ *teaspoon nutmeg*
salt and pepper

Combine the ingredients and simmer for 15 minutes. Serve over rice with side dishes of chutney and coconut.

Pork

Pork roasts usually come with the bones cut part way through, so little effort is required to remove several chops and thus reduce the size of the initial roast. Reserve the roast for a special occasion and start, in true Poor Poet style, with this homesy-folksy dish.

PORK CHOPS AND BABY TURNIPS ∾ 4

4 *pork chops*
1 *tablespoon butter*
4 *young turnips*
½ *cup dry white wine*
salt and pepper
chopped parsley

Brown the chops in butter. Quarter and add the turnips, wine, salt, and pepper. Cover and cook over low heat for 30 minutes or until the turnips are tender and the meat is done. Serve sprinkled with chopped parsley.

PORK CHOPS WITH BEER ∾ 6

6 *thick pork chops*
1 *clove garlic*
1 *tablespoon butter*
2 *onions, sliced*
2 *apples, sliced*
2 *tablespoons flour*
1 *tablespoon each minced parsley and chives*
2 *cups beer*
salt and pepper
pinch of cayenne

Rub a skillet with garlic, add the butter, onions, and apples, and brown. Put these in a casserole. Now brown the chops and place them on top of the onion-apple mixture. Stir the flour into the fat remaining in the pan; add the parsley and chives, and gradually stir in the beer. When the sauce is smooth, season to taste, and pour it over the meat. Bake for 1 hour at 350°.

SUNDAY LOIN OF PORK WITH LIMAS 6–8

1 *pound dry lima beans*
4 *teaspoons salt*
4 *pounds loin of pork*
2 *large onions*
2 *bay leaves*
¼ *cup brown sugar*
¼ *teaspoon pepper*

Cover the limas with water and soak overnight. (A sprinkling of unseasoned meat tenderizer will speed up the forthcoming cooking time.) Drain, cover with fresh water and 2 teaspoons salt, and cook over low heat for about an hour.

In the meantime, salt and roast the pork in a 325° oven for 1 hour (30 minutes per pound). When the meat is half done, spoon drained beans around the roast along with ½ cup of the bean liquid, onions peeled and cut in wedges, and other ingredients. Continue roasting until the meat is done, checking every so often that there is a bit of liquid in the bottom of the pan.

ROAST PORK, TROPICAL STYLE 6

4 *pounds loin of pork*
  soy sauce, garlic, ginger, salt, and pepper
6 *bananas*

Rub the seasonings well into the pork, and let stand for about an hour. Roast in a 325° oven at 30 minutes per pound. About a half hour before serving time peel the bananas and cut in half cross-wise. Lay them around the roast where they will cook in the drippings to a golden brown.

PORK SATE

An exciting combination that was initially whipped up as a marinade for bits of pork that would be roasted over charcoal. Then it was used on spareribs with great success. Finally, a loin of pork was rubbed and soaked in the same mixture, then roasted in the oven, with excellent results. Ingredients listed are sufficient for 1½ pounds of pork.

4 tablespoons peanut butter
2 tablespoons ground coriander
1 teaspoon salt
1 teaspoon black pepper
2 or 3 onions
2 cloves garlic
1 teaspoon lemon juice
2 tablespoons brown sugar
4 tablespoons soy sauce
1 chili pepper, seeded
2 or 3 tablespoons salad oil

Chop the onions and garlic and then mash all the ingredients to a paste, using a mortar, chopping bowl, or (what luck) electric blender.

Veal

May, splendid in new green grass and flowers, is calf time in the cattle country. This means Poor Poet-priced veal in abundance in all the markets.

A 4- to 5-pound rump roast will make a boneless roast for six with enough slices for a completely different dinner, PLUS a small bone for soup. Merely cut the necessary number of slices from the full end of the rump. (These may later be pounded quite thin.) This will expose the hipbone, which is easy to cut around and remove.

VEAL ROAST WITH PAPRIKA   ∾ 6–8

3- to 4-pound boned veal rump
1 large onion
½ teaspoon salt
2 teaspoons paprika
⅛ teaspoon pepper
½ pound fat salt pork

Peel and chop the onion and stuff it into the cavity from the blade bone. Fold meat over, and tie with string. Rub salt, paprika, and pepper well into the roast. Now slice the salt pork and lay the strips over the roast. They should be fastened down with toothpicks. Roast the veal in a slow oven (325°) at 30 minutes per pound.

This roast is excellent served with noodles that have been tossed with a handful of chopped parsley. A squeeze of lemon juice or a grating of lemon rind added to the veal gravy is interesting. Brandy is fascinating.

VEAL ROAST DIJON   ∾ 6–8

3- to 4-pound boned veal rump roast
salt and pepper
¼ cup Dijon mustard
½ stick butter
dry white wine or chicken stock

Salt and pepper the veal and place it in a roasting pan. Cream together the mustard and butter, and spread half this on the meat. Roast at 300° at 40 minutes per pound, basting often with the pan juices and adding wine or stock as necessary. When the roast is half done, spread it with the rest of the mustard-butter mixture. Serve with buttered noodles and the pan juices.

VEAL, HONORED GUESTS ℘ 8

3½ *pounds veal stew meat*
2 *cloves garlic*
⅛ *pound butter*
1 *heaping tablespoon tomato preserves or currant jelly*
2 *tablespoons dry vermouth*
1 *cup dry white wine*
2 *big tablespoons parsley*
1 *cup chicken stock*
½ *pound mushrooms*

Freeze the meat and then cut in thin slices. Dry well and brown in butter. Place the meat in a baking dish. Brown garlic slivers in the butter and reserve them. Brown the flour slightly and then add preserves, wines, and stock. Blend and thicken. Now add parsley, garlic, and sliced mushrooms. Pour this sauce over the veal, cover, and bake an hour or so at 375°.

VEAL ROSEMARY ℘ 4

2 *pounds veal stew meat*
1 *cup white port*
¾ *cup cream*
5 *tablespoons butter*
2 *cloves garlic*
1 *teaspoon crushed rosemary*
½ *pound mushrooms*
   salt, pepper, and flour

Freeze, slice, and dry the veal. Slice mushrooms and brown in butter. Reserve. Simmer garlic in butter and discard the cloves. Now back to the meat. Flour it, and brown well. Then add the wine, cover, and simmer 1 hour. Then it is time to stir in the mushrooms, rosemary, and cream. Season with salt and a little pepper. Taste to see how everything is progressing, and allow the dish to cook for 10 minutes longer. Veal Rosemary definitely requires buttered noodles.

VEAL VERONICA 4

A nice solution for people who, like Veronica, maintain kitchens the size of hall closets.

4 thin veal steaks
1 tablespoon butter
1 can condensed cream of mushroom soup
½ cup dry white wine

Pound the steaks into thin, uniform pieces, and brown in butter. Combine soup and wine and spoon over the steaks. Cover and simmer gently for 45 minutes. Instant mashed potatoes, a jar of pickled peaches, and a salad are workable accompaniments for the minuscule kitchen.

VEAL WITH MUSHROOMS 4

A rich dish!

2 pounds veal, thinly sliced
butter
½ pound mushrooms
1 cup heavy cream
1 jigger brandy
salt and pepper
flour
1 cup water

Roll veal in flour and brown in butter, then remove meat. Pour 1 cup of water into the remaining butter and veal juices and simmer this sauce to reduce it. Slice mushrooms, put them in a second pan with a lump of butter, and toss for about 5 minutes over medium heat. The mushrooms now go over the meat. And over both go the sauce and the cream, along with a little salt and pepper. Cover and place in a 375° oven for 20 minutes. Add the brandy just before serving.

Ground Beef

Ground beef was invented for Poor Poets. Especially the least expensive regular grind when funds are short. When they are not, he can graduate to ground chuck; splurge on ground round.

Then, when funds are holding their own, there is the coarse single grind to consider. Use of the latter, often packaged in supermarkets as "ground beef for chili," results in extra juicy, tender hamburger steaks. Because this grind is not at all compact, it makes meat loaves and meat balls that fall apart. Beware.

Ground beef delights Poor Poets because it can be used in divers ways. It is inadvisable but, with some imagination, a complete ground beef dinner could be devised. It might start with appetizers of cocktail-size meat balls to be dipped in cheese sauce. Following that would be bowls of minestrone-hamburger soup. And then might come spaghetti, or lasagna, or even stuffed peppers or cabbage rolls. The whole could always be topped off by a mincemeat some-thing-or-other. But this last might tip the scale too far, and the poet would forever lose his taste for ground beef. A sad situation indeed.

Because many of the One Pots with Meat rely heavily on ground beef, let us here consider only three or four things. First is:

A HAMBURGER SANDWICH

This hamburger sandwich is not one encased in bread or a roll. It is a filling sandwiched between two thin patties of hamburger. It is served on a plate. Only if the latter is missing, or if one is going walking, is a bread covering allowed.

Figure on one pound of hamburger for every four persons. For each serving pat the meat into two equal-size discs. Pile whatever filling desired on one disc. Top it with the other, seal the edges, and broil the meat.

Or—

If the hamburgers are sautéed in a skillet, a further step can be taken. As soon as the meat is removed, splash a little red wine, brandy, bourbon, or rum into the pan. (If the pan is very hot this maneuver will cause great spitting and possibly some blue flames.) Stir the sauce for perhaps a minute and pour it over the meat.

Hamburger sauce-making has a dual purpose. Flavor, of course. Furthermore, it tends to remove a lot of the meat particles stuck in the pan—contributing to easier dish washing.

Now, to the stuffing possibilities.

LOTS of paprika
Prepared mustard and sliced dill pickle
Sunflower seeds or toasted sesame seeds
Leftover beans
Diced salami, ham, or cooked bacon
Cheese and a slice of green chili
Potato salad
Chutney and flaked coconut
Chive or vegetable cottage cheese
Green onions, caraway seeds, and vinegar
Pickled beets
Chopped black or green pimiento-stuffed olives

A LARGE MEAT BALL ↻ 4

This is a make-in-the-cool-of-the-morning-and-eat-at-the-end-of-a-hot-day dish. It also has a by-product: soup stock.

1½ *pounds ground beef*
4 *slices bread*
1 *egg*
2 *tablespoons Parmesan cheese*
1 *heaping teaspoon chopped parsley*
1 *teaspoon crushed basil*
¼ *teaspoon salt*

2 *quarts water*
1 *stalk celery with leaves*
1 *large onion*
1 *large carrot*
1 *tomato or a big tablespoon of tomato paste*
2 *stalks parsley*
dash of salt

Soak the bread in some water or wine, squeeze dry, and crumble into the meat. Now add the egg, cheese, parsley, basil, and salt; mix well and form into one large meat ball. Shroud the meat ball in cheesecloth and immerse it in the boiling soup stock that's been made from the remaining ingredients. Lower the heat and simmer for 2 hours.

Remove the meat to a plate, discard the cheesecloth, and let the meat ball drain and cool. Tuck it in the refrigerator until ready to serve cold with a caper sauce:

2 *tablespoons capers*
6 *anchovy fillets*
　olive oil
　juice of one lemon
　cracked pepper

Pound the capers and anchovies in a mortar, adding olive oil little by little until there is about a cup of sauce. Finish with the lemon juice and pepper. But no salt; the anchovies take care of that. This sauce is also excellent with fish.

KID STUFF ♋ 4

This is on the sweet side, so very appropriate for children. Adults like it, too.

1 *pound ground beef*	$\frac{1}{8}$ *teaspoon pepper*
1 *small onion*	$\frac{1}{2}$ *cup chili sauce*
1 *teaspoon chili powder*	4 *strips bacon*
1 *teaspoon salt*	4 *canned apricot halves*

Chop the onion and combine gently with ground beef, chili powder, salt, pepper, and chili sauce. Form into four patties, wrap a wall of bacon around each, and fasten with a toothpick. Top each with an apricot half. Now bake in a hot, 450° oven for 20 to 25 minutes.

HAMBURGER, RED FLANNEL STYLE ♋ 6

1$\frac{1}{2}$ *pounds ground beef*	1 *medium onion*
1 *cup mashed potatoes*	2 *tablespoons capers*
1 *egg*	1 *teaspoon salt*
$\frac{1}{2}$ *cup evaporated milk*	$\frac{1}{2}$ *teaspoon pepper*
$\frac{1}{2}$ *cup chopped pickled beets*	*chopped parsley*

Chop the onions and capers with the pickled beets. Combine everything but the parsley and mix thoroughly. Now pat out twelve little steaks or six big ones. Sauté these in butter and sprinkle with parsley just before serving. Some sort of pickled fruit goes nicely on the side.

Variety Meats

The Poor Poet of the Orient dries and pulverizes the variety meats, sprinkling them over assorted dishes for an energy boost. His colleague directly across the Pacific buys the same meats canned or fresh, feeding them to his sleek cat and purchasing vitamins regularly.

This brief section is therefore designed for the squeamish ("I'd *never* touch—") as an introduction to an interesting assortment of viands.

HEART

Veal hearts, which weigh about a pound each (one will serve two people), are the best choice. Beef hearts, which are three or four times larger, are less expensive, though tougher. They can be bought sliced, and after cutting away the veins and hard parts, should be soaked overnight in buttermilk or water and lemon juice. After cooking, beef hearts should be served immediately, for they will toughen if allowed to stand.

Whole beef hearts can be stuffed, tied, and cooked as a pot roast. Ground beef heart can be mixed with pork sausage, seasoned with garlic, thyme, nutmeg, marjoram, and sage and otherwise prepared as a meat loaf.

Sliced beef heart makes a fine steak.

BEEF HEART STEAKS ❧ 4

2 *pounds beef heart*	1 *large clove garlic*
olive oil	*juice of one lemon*
salt and pepper	*chopped parsley*

Tenderize the heart as noted above, or use a meat tenderizer. Dry the meat, slice thin, and marinate in $\frac{1}{4}$ cup olive oil, $\frac{1}{2}$ teaspoon salt, and $\frac{1}{4}$ teaspoon pepper for at least 30 minutes.

Sauté one clove of garlic in 3 or 4 tablespoons of olive oil and discard. Now add the heart and brown it well on both sides over high heat. Continue to cook for 8 minutes, turning the slices frequently. Serve sprinkled with salt, pepper, lemon juice, and chopped parsley.

SKEWERED BEEF HEART ☙ 6

2 *pounds beef heart*
6 *peppercorns*
1 *crumbled chili teppin*
   pinch of saffron
3 *cloves garlic, minced*
1 *cup vinegar*
½ *cup water*

Cut the heart in 1-inch cubes and marinate overnight in the other ingredients. Drain well, skewer, brush with a little oil, and broil in the fireplace or even the oven until the meat is tender. Serve the skewers on a bed of brown rice.

LIVER

Lamb liver is too dry; calves' liver is too dear. Pork liver is the best buy, with that from beef running a close second.

LIVER WITH LEMON AND PARSLEY ☙ 2

1 *pound pork liver*
   juice of one lemon
2 *heaping tablespoons chopped parsley*
   salt and pepper

Marinate the liver in lemon and parsley for about an hour. Sauté in butter and serve sprinkled with additional parsley, salt, and pepper. Good with mashed potatoes, and a good gravy can be made from the fat and scraps in the pan.

NANKING LIVER II ♋ 4

1 *pound liver*
2 *tablespoons soy sauce*
1 *tablespoon sherry*
1 *teaspoon freshly grated ginger root*
2 *bunches green onions*
3 *tablespoons salad oil*

Cut the liver in narrow strips and marinate in the soy sauce, sherry, and ginger root for 10 minutes or longer. In the meantime, thinly slice the green onions. Bring the oil to a bubble in a heavy frying pan. Toss in the slightly drained liver and cook for 1 or 2 minutes, stirring constantly with a fork or chopsticks. Add the onions and cook only until they are tender-crisp. Steamed rice accompanies this. Or, for a change, warm flour tortillas.

OXTAILS

Economical and rich in flavor and protein is the whip-like oxtail, revered in mythology for its strength and wisdom. Disjointed, not hacked up aimlessly with a cleaver, and well browned, the pieces make superb soups or stews.

OXTAILS VERMOUTH ♋ 6

4½ *pounds disjointed oxtails*
1 *or 2 tablespoons shortening*
½ *cup chopped celery*
¾ *cup chopped onions*
1 *large clove garlic*
⅛ *teaspoon rosemary*
⅛ *teaspoon thyme*
1 *teaspoon salt*
½ *teaspoon pepper*
1 *cup dry vermouth*
4 *cups water*
1½ *cups sliced mushrooms*
½ *cup sliced stuffed green olives*
2 *tablespoons cornstarch*

Brown oxtails in a heavy pan and then brown the vegetables. Add the herbs, salt, pepper, vermouth, and water. Cover tightly and simmer in a 325° oven for 2 to 2½ hours. Now toss in the mushrooms and olives and continue cooking for another half hour. Skim excess fat and thicken with cornstarch mixed with a little water.

This is a rich dish, and anything left over seems even better the next day.

BEEF TONGUE—BON VIVANT   6

1 4-*pound fresh beef tongue*	1½ *cups tomato sauce*
	salt and pepper
2 *tablespoons butter*	2 *tablespoons chopped parsley*
2 *tablespoons oil*	
1 *onion*	1 *clove garlic*
2 *carrots*	3 *tablespoons pickle relish*
1½ *cups dry white wine*	½ *teaspoon oregano*

Cover tongue with water and simmer 2 hours. Remove, cool, and skin. Brown tongue in butter and oil with chopped onion and carrot. Add wine, tomato sauce, salt, and pepper. Simmer covered 1 hour. Remove tongue. Skim excess fat, stir in remaining ingredients, and simmer 5 minutes. Pour sauce over sliced tongue.

SAUSAGES

Sausages are neat little packages with numerous advantages: i.e., much, if not all, of the cooking has been done; they generally keep longer than other meats; there is variety almost without end.

NATIONAL HOLIDAY BRATWURST

In many Swiss towns the national holiday is celebrated with parades and fireworks. Poets read odes, writers publish tributes, and musicians play far into the night for costumed dancers. Throughout the day everyone eats bratwurst.

Allow one bratwurst per serving. Slash it three times on each side. Broil gently over charcoal. Serve on French bread with lots of mustard. Beer is a must.

SAUSAGES IN WHITE WINE ♋ 4

1½ *pounds pork sausages*
1 *cup consommé*
1½ *cups dry white wine*
1 *stalk celery*
1 *large carrot*
   chopped parsley or green onion tops

Parboil the sausages and drain. Chop the vegetables as fine as possible. Combine all ingredients except the parsley and simmer for 15 to 20 minutes. If desired, thicken the sauce with a little flour. Serve with mashed potatoes, and use a lavish sprinkling of parsley to avoid an anemic dish. Furthermore, never serve Sausages in White Wine on white plates.

POOR POETS TURKEY SAUSAGE ♋ 4

The Poor Poet desiring something more original (and often more economical) than store-bought sausages is encouraged to experiment with the following.

1 *pound freshly ground fresh turkey*	½ *teaspoon pepper*
	¼ *teaspoon powdered sage*
¼ *teaspoon sugar*	½ *tablespoon grated ginger root*
1 *teaspoon salt*	

Mix all the ingredients, shape into patties, wrap, and refrigerate until ready to use. To cook, brown the patties on both sides, then cover and continue cooking 5 to 10 minutes.

ET CETERA

POINDEXTER SCRAPPLE   ೭ 4–6

1 *cup hominy grits*
1 *pound bulk pork sausage*
3 *large eggs*

Cook the grits as directed on the package and, in the meantime, fry and crumble the sausage. Drain it well and beat into the cooked grits along with the three eggs. Pour into a buttered mold and chill. Slice the scrapple and brown in lots of butter. Serve awash with maple syrup.

BAJA CALIFORNIA SCRAPPLE   ೭ 4–6

½ *pound bacon or salt pork*
2 *large onions*
1 *large clove garlic*
1¼ *cups cornmeal*
½ *teaspoon chili powder*
¼ *teaspoon oregano*
¼ *teaspoon cumin*
¼ *cup sliced stuffed green olives*

Dice the bacon, onions, and garlic, brown well, and reserve. Cook the cornmeal and spices in a double boiler, following directions on cornmeal package. In about 45 minutes, at which time the cornmeal should be done, add the browned bacon-onions and the olives. Stir well, pour into a greased, 1-quart mold, and chill. The scrapple is now ready to slice and fry. It goes fine with eggs or applesauce.

VARIETY MEATS

POOR POET'S PASTRAMI   ❦ 8–10

4 pounds corned beef
4 tablespoons liquid smoke sauce
4 large cloves garlic
1 enormous onion
2 tablespoons pickling spices
6 to 8 tablespoons coarsely ground pepper

Rub the corned beef with 2 tablespoons liquid smoke sauce, wrap closely in foil, and refrigerate overnight. The next day unwrap the meat and simmer it, along with the garlic, onion, pickling spices, and the remaining 2 tablespoons liquid smoke sauce, in water to cover for 2½ hours. (It is not necessary to peel the garlic, although the onion should be peeled and cut in large hunks.) Cool the meat in the broth, then remove, pat dry with paper towels, and rub pepper all over the surface, building up a layer thick enough that little meat shows through. Encase the pastrami in aluminum foil and store in the refrigerator for at least 2 days. Slice *very* thin to serve.

Chicken

In the thirties poultry producers happened upon the battery-raising method used by the early Romans, improved upon it, and ever since the possibility of "a chicken in every pot" has been a reality.

Not only that, but the experts tell us that chicken is low in calories, high in protein, and pound for pound always an excellent buy.

So the problem posed the Poor Poet is not "Shall we have chicken?" but "*How* shall we have it?"

POOR POET'S CHICKEN ☙ 4

1 *whole frying chicken*
2 or 3 *large cloves garlic*
juice of 2 *lemons*
salt
freshly cracked pepper

Place the chicken in a roasting pan, slide it into the oven, and roast at 325° until the chicken is tender (45 minutes to an hour). In the meantime, mash the garlic in a mortar and then mix in the lemon juice, a scant teaspoon salt, and at least a half teaspoon cracked pepper.

When the chicken is done, cut it up on a serving platter and pour over it the garlic-lemon sauce along with any juice from the pan. This is good with rice, or with crisp rolls that can be dunked into the juice.

OVEN-BROILED CHICKEN

Broiler-fryer chickens split, washed, dried, and variously seasoned, are broiled—skin side down—in a hot (450°) oven for about 45 minutes. The halves are juicy on the inside and have exceptionally crisp skin. Figure roughly on half a 2-pound chicken per person.

Chicken parts—even backbones for the poor Poor Poet—can be treated in this manner. But shorten the cooking time! In fact, if there is no oven, the chicken can be fried. And, if there is no stove at all, it can be done in the fireplace or barbecue or campfire.

HERB-SMOTHERED CHICKEN

Rub chicken halves with a bit of oil or butter and mashed garlic. Sprinkle liberally with salt, pepper, paprika, rosemary, and basil or oregano.

CHICKEN D'ORO

2 tablespoons melted butter
1 large orange
2 teaspoons paprika
salt and pepper

Coat the chicken halves with butter. Then pat each half with grated orange rind, paprika, salt, and pepper. Squeeze orange juice over the chicken two or three times while it is broiling.

PHOENIX

Proceed as for Herb-Smothered Chicken. When ready to serve, bed the chicken on a platter of celery leaves or similar greenery dusted with paprika. Heat $\frac{1}{4}$ cup light or golden rum, ignite, and pour over the chicken.

CHICKEN DIJON

Dijon-style mustard
garlic salt
Herbes de Provence (See page 201).

Spread a thin (or thick, if one is a mustard addict) coat of mustard over the chicken. Shake on a good amount of garlic salt, and then pat the *herbes* over the skin side.

CHICKEN WITH YOGURT AND PARMESAN

$\frac{1}{2}$ cup yogurt
1 clove garlic, crushed
4 tablespoons Parmesan cheese
salt and pepper
$\frac{1}{2}$ stick butter

Rub the chicken with yogurt and garlic and allow to stand for several hours. Now dust the pieces with salt, pepper, and grated Parmesan. Melt butter in the baking pan before adding the chicken. Baste several times during broiling.

CHICKEN WITH YOGURT AND SPICES

½ *cup yogurt*
1 *teaspoon salt*
1 *clove garlic, crushed*
½ *teaspoon cardamom*

½ *teaspoon chili powder*
¼ *teaspoon cinnamon*
¼ *teaspoon ginger*

Combine all the ingredients, pour over the chicken, and marinate in the refrigerator for 2 hours at the very least. Broil.

Because yogurt acts as a tenderizer, this is a wise method to follow when one is in doubt as to the age of the chicken.

CHICKEN, AQUARIUM STYLE II

A baker's dozen years later and the story that prompted the original recipe still fascinates. To wit:

A lady visiting a nearby aquarium not long ago had her purse snapped up by an alligator. After 2 hours of contented chewing, while being tapped on the head with a long pole (this is said to make alligators spit), he forfeited the bag—contents intact except for a package of lemon drops.

This led to contemplation of the value of pre-lemon-flavored alligator meat, and because these creatures are said to taste like chicken, of the value of seasoning the latter with lemon or lime.

3 *limes*
1 *tablespoon chopped parsley*

1 *tablespoon chopped capers*
salt and pepper

Squeeze the limes, mix with other ingredients, and use to marinate the chicken for at least an hour before broiling.

FRIED CHICKEN

FRIED CHICKEN WITH SESAME   ∞ 4

- 1 3½–4-pound chicken, cut for frying
- 1 egg
- ½ cup milk
- ½ cup flour
- ½ teaspoon baking powder
- 2 teaspoons paprika
- 2 teaspoons salt
- 1 teaspoon pepper
- ¼ cup finely chopped peanuts
- ¼ cup sesame seeds
- 1 stick butter or ¼ cup shortening

Beat the egg and milk together. Dip chicken pieces into this and then into flour mixed with baking powder, salt, pepper, paprika, nuts, and sesame seeds. (Although shaking chicken and seasoned flour together in a paper bag is generally the best idea, it doesn't work well here, as the nuts and seeds tend to remain off the chicken and in the bag.)

Fry the chicken until it is nicely browned. Add a tablespoon or two of water and cover the pan loosely. Cook over low heat for about 45 minutes or until chicken is tender.

If gravy is called for, add 1½ cups milk to drippings in pan and heat to scalding. Mix 4 tablespoons flour with an additional ½ cup milk, add to the pan, and cook, stirring constantly until the gravy is thick and smooth. Season with salt, pepper, lots of paprika, and a good dash of sherry.

CHICKEN IN A POT

CHICKEN FRICASSÉE   ୯ 4–5

1 4–5-pound stewing hen	½ bay leaf
2 cups water	dash of thyme
2 cups dry white wine	6 crushed juniper berries
1½ teaspoons salt	or ¼ cup gin
1 large carrot	3 tablespoons flour
1 large onion	½ cup thin cream
3 or 4 sprigs parsley and celery tops	2 egg yolks
	1 cup hot cooked peas

Bring water, 1 cup wine, salt, cut-up vegetables, the juniper berries or gin, and herbs to a boil. Plunk in the chicken, cover, and simmer until tender. This will take about 2 hours, but cooking time can be considerably cut if frying chickens are substituted for stewing hens.

When the chicken is done, remove it and keep hot. Discard the vegetables and skim excess fat. Pour in the remaining cup of wine, reheat, and thicken with flour mixed with cream and egg yolks. Return the chicken to the pot, along with the peas, and let the fricassée heat well throughout. Great with mashed potatoes.

CHICKEN SCALLOPINI   ୯ 4–6

2 pounds chicken breasts	¾ cup dry white wine
2 tablespoons each butter and oil	1½ teaspoons lemon juice
	¼ teaspoon Italian herbs
1½ cups sliced mushrooms	1 tablespoon chopped parsley
1 small clove garlic, crushed	salt and pepper

Skin and bone the breasts, place on waxed paper, and pound gently until each is more than doubled in size.

CHICKEN

Brown (just to bisque color) the meat in the butter and oil, remove, and keep warm. Add garlic and mushrooms to the pan, sauté a minute, and add the other ingredients along with the chicken. Simmer just to heat through.

Turkey breasts respond well to this method. Bone and skin the breasts, place meat in the freezer for about 45 minutes, and cut in $\frac{1}{4}$-inch slices.

CHICKEN EDGEWOOD 4–6

2 *frying chickens, 2–2$\frac{1}{2}$-pounds*
$\frac{1}{2}$ *cup flour*
2 *teaspoons salt*
1 *teaspoon garlic powder*
1 *teaspoon pepper*
$\frac{1}{2}$ *cup shortening*
2 *bananas*
1 *pound yams, parboiled*
2 *large oranges*
4 *or 5 chili teppins*
$\frac{1}{2}$ *teaspoon nutmeg*
$\frac{1}{2}$ *cup chopped parsley*

Shake cut-up chicken, flour, garlic powder, salt, and pepper together in a paper bag. Brown the chicken well in hot shortening, add 2 or 3 tablespoons of water, cover the skillet loosely, and cook over low heat for 30 minutes.

Quarter the bananas and unpeeled oranges, and cut the yams in thick slabs. Seed and crush the chilies. Add all these, along with nutmeg, to the chicken. Re-cover and continue cooking until the chicken is done, about 15 minutes. Serve strewn with parsley. Rice is the preferred side dish.

LEFTOVER CHICKEN

Well, there's always creamed chicken (or turkey) but here are two with a difference.

CORAL CHICKEN   ᘌ 6

- ½ *small onion, minced*
- ¼ *cup butter*
- 1 *cup sliced mushrooms (preferably fresh, but drained if canned)*
- 1 *teaspoon paprika*
- 1 *teaspoon salt*
- ¼ *teaspoon nutmeg*
- 6 *slices cooked chicken white meat*
- 6 *slices cooked ham*
- 1½ *cups rich milk (or 1 cup milk and ½ cup chicken stock)*
- ¼ *cup dry white wine or light sherry*
- 4 *tablespoons grated Parmesan cheese*

Melt the butter in a baking dish and sauté the onion until it is tender. Add mushrooms and seasonings and cook for 5 minutes. Lay the slices of chicken and ham on the mushroom bed and nearly drown with milk and wine.

Bake in a 400° oven for 10 minutes, sprinkle with grated cheese, and return to the oven to brown.

AMIGO II   ᘌ 4–6

So named because more chicken, chili, cheese, or tortillas may be added without noticeably affecting the taste but noticeably increasing the number of servings,

1 *onion, chopped*
2 *cups leftover chicken*
1 *4-ounce can chopped green chilies*
½ *cup raisins*
½ *cup chopped ripe olives*
1 *10-ounce can enchilada sauce*
1 *cup grated cheese*
1 *dozen corn tortillas*

Stir together everything but the cheese and tortillas. Lay three or four tortillas in the bottom of a buttered baking dish and top with part of the chicken mixture and a sprinkling of cheese. Continue layering. Bake for 30 to 35 minutes at 350°.

Amigo can be stretched even further with the addition of a can of whole-kernel corn, drained.

WINGS, LIVERS, AND GIBLETS AS CHOICE ITEMS

Smiling bravely, someone will claim, "But I *like* backbones"—or wingtips, necks, gizzards. Paltry fare, at best, if consumed in lieu of a fat drumstick. However, given individual treatment, the less choice parts become very choice indeed.

Congee, the thick rice soup (page 15), is one cold-weather answer. Spaghetti sauce made from giblets instead of ground beef is another. Then there are dishes calling for a fair quantity of a specific part; ingredients are come by either through patience and freezer-storage or a visit to a poultry market.

CHICKEN WINGS AND PLUMS   ℧ 4

3 *pounds chicken wings*
1 *medium onion*
1 *clove garlic*
1 *tablespoon pickling spices*
½ *teaspoon dry mustard*
1 *one-pound can purple plums*
½ *teaspoon salt*
2 *tablespoons wine vinegar*

Cut the onion into rings. Tie the garlic and spices in a cheesecloth bag. Combine these with the plums and their syrup, the mustard, salt, and vinegar in a saucepan. Heat just to boiling. Cool and refrigerate overnight. Remove plums and onion rings and strain the marinade over the wings. Allow them to steep all day. Broil for 30 to 45 minutes at 450°, turning and basting frequently.

Serve the marinated plums and onion rings with the wings. Rice or buttered noodles go well with this.

CHICKEN GIBLETS AND VERMICELLI   ℧ 4

1 *pound chicken giblets*
2 *tablespoons olive oil*
2 *large onions*
2 or 3 *large tomatoes*
1 *teaspoon salt*
¼ *teaspoon pepper*
1 *teaspoon paprika*
¼ *teaspoon each thyme and marjoram*
½ *cup water*
¾ *pound vermicelli*

Chop giblets slightly and, reserving the livers, brown along with chopped onions in olive oil. Add the coarsely chopped tomatoes, seasonings, and water. Cover and simmer about an hour or until the giblets are tender. Add the livers about 10 minutes before the giblets are done.

In the meantime, toast vermicelli in the oven until it is a light golden color. Boil in salted water until soft, drain, and combine with the sauce. Simmer to heat through.

A green salad with olive oil, red wine, and crusty bread accompany this dish.

SAUTÉED CHICKEN GIBLETS ↺ 4

A Poor Poet who lived several miles from the nearest store was all set to make chicken giblet kabobs when it was discovered there were no skewers. There wasn't even a new broom from which substitute sticks could be made. And that is how Sautéed Chicken Giblets came about.

1 *pound chicken giblets*
4 *tablespoons butter*
1 *onion*
1 *or 2 green peppers*
½ *pound mushrooms*
12 *cherry tomatoes*
½ *cup dry sherry*
salt and pepper
2 *tablespoons chopped parsley*

(If gizzards are used, simmer them for an hour, or until tender.) Melt the butter and brown the giblets over low heat. Cut the onion and pepper into chunks. Add them to the giblets and cook and stir a minute or two. Slice the mushrooms and add with the other ingredients. Simmer to heat through. Serve with rice or French bread and butter.

CHICKEN LIVERS, SWEET AND PUNGENT ↺ 4

1 *pound chicken livers*
2 *tablespoons oil*
1 *cup chicken bouillon*
4 *slices canned pineapple*
3 *large green peppers, seeds removed*
3 *tablespoons cornstarch*
2 *teaspoons soy sauce*
½ *cup cider vinegar*
½ *cup sugar*
salt and pepper

Cut the livers in two pieces each and cook quickly in hot fat, with a little salt and pepper, until light brown. Remove and keep warm. Add ⅓ cup bouillon, cut-up pineapple and peppers, cover, and simmer 5 minutes.

Mix the cornstarch, soy sauce, vinegar, sugar, and ⅔ cup bouillon. Add to the other ingredients and cook and stir for 5 minutes, or until the sauce is thick and clear. Pour sauce over the livers and serve with rice.

RUMAKI   ଓ 2–4

Rumaki take care and patience to make. They are meant for someone who is loved.

1 *pound chicken livers*   ⅓ *cup sherry*
1 *can water chestnuts*   3 *tablespoons soy sauce*
½ *pound thin-sliced bacon*   *bamboo skewers*

Cut each liver in two pieces and dip in boiling water so they are easier to work with. Cook the bacon until it is just limp and drain. Drain and slice the water chestnuts. Get out the skewers, and it is time to begin. Place a chestnut slice on each side of a piece of liver, wrap with bacon, and skewer. When all the Rumaki are so made, place them in a dish and drench with soy sauce and sherry. Let them soak for several hours, turning them occasionally.

Broil them over charcoal or in a 500° oven for 5 minutes. Serve them as hors d'œuvres or as an entrée with steamed rice.

BREADS

Third grade was a pinecone turkey at Thanksgiving and red and green paper chains at Christmas. It was percussion band and flash card and planting a tree each Arbor Day.

It was a sand table with little toy trucks and houses and a field in which real wheat grew.

It was Columbus and Magellan; but the only thing that remains distinct (and in the lower right page of the history book) is the picture of the last boy of Pompeii and his faithful dog. And next to the picture was a description of the boy's house and how the dishes were found, so much later, still on the table, along with a loaf of bread.

Today's bread doesn't keep quite that long, even with the addition of preservatives and fortifiers. Here are a few things to do with bread that's stood on the shelf many days—but not so many that it is shrouded in soft powdery blue mold.*

---

*Not to be overlooked are Poor Poet's Soufflé, Bread Pudding, croutons for soups and salads, and bread crumbs to feed to the birds in the park.

Glorifying Store Bread

ANISE TOAST

Lay thin slices of bread on a baking sheet. Sprinkle a little water over the slices and pat on a few anise seeds. Bake the bread at 300° until crisp and lightly browned.

PULLED BREAD

Use some care in pulling the insides from loaves used to make Breadloaves (page 136). Break the bread into serving-size pieces. Brush with melted butter and bake at 325° until crisp and brown. Pulled Bread can be used in place of rolls or crackers with salad or soup. The smaller pieces can be used for croutons.

MAPLE TOAST

Dip slices of bread in maple syrup and sauté in butter until light brown. Care must be taken so that the syrup candies but does not burn.

RUM TOAST

Make a syrup of brown sugar or honey—even tag ends of jelly—and rum. Dip slices of bread in the syrup and proceed as for Maple Toast.

CRUNCH!

Combine equal parts of melted butter, honey, granola-type cereal, and grated coconut, plus some sesame seeds. Lay slices of lightly toasted bread on a baking sheet, spread with the Crunch mixture, and place in a hot oven or under the broiler until the topping is crisp and golden.

CUSTARD TOAST ℘ 2–3

There are many French toasts, but this one is far superior.

6 *fairly thick slices of bread*
2 *eggs*
1 *cup rich milk*
1 *teaspoon sugar*
½ *teaspoon vanilla*
¼ *teaspoon nutmeg*
  lots of butter

Beat together the eggs, milk, sugar, vanilla, and nutmeg. Dip slices of bread into the mixture, allowing each slice to soak in as much liquid as possible.

Sauté slowly in butter, turning once. The outside should be crisp while the inside is reminiscent of custard. Serve with syrup, jam, or a dusting of powdered sugar.

The addition of ¼ teaspoon baking powder to the liquid will make the toast even fluffier.

Pulled bread can be used for Custard Toast. In this case fry in hot deep fat (365°–375°).

BREAD AND WINE

1 *long loaf French bread*
⅓ *cup soft butter*
¼ *cup claret or Burgundy wine*
  dash of salt and cayenne

Slash the loaf into thick slices, cutting almost to the bottom crust. Beat the wine, salt, and cayenne into the butter and spread between slices and over the top of the loaf.

Bake for 10 minutes at 400°. This is a welcome change from garlic bread, especially when garlic has been used with a lavish hand in accompanying dishes.

HERMIT GARLIC BREAD

The poet, or painter, or anyone who desires a few days' solitude is admonished to first dine on Hermit Bread. Red wine is good for washing down. The bread is also an excellent accompaniment to a thick soup and/or salad.

1 *long leaf French bread*
4 *tablespoons soft butter*
4 *large cloves garlic*
¼ *cup sherry*
1 *cup grated Parmesan cheese*

Slash the loaf, almost to the bottom crust. Mash the garlic and mix with the other ingredients. Spread the mixture between the slices, with a little saved for the top. Put the bread in a paper bag and sprinkle water over the bag. Bake 15 to 20 minutes at 350°. When the paper bag is crisp and beginning to brown the loaf is done.

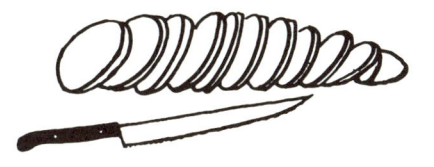

OLIVE TILES

10 *slices day-old bread*
1 *cup chopped black olives*
1 *egg*
¼ *cup chopped onion*
2½ *cups grated Cheddar cheese*
  several dashes Tabasco
⅓ *cup olive oil or melted butter*

Beat the egg lightly and stir in the oil, onion, cheese, Tabasco, and olives. Lay the slices of bread on a lightly oiled baking pan and spread with the topping. Bake for 15 to 20 minutes at 400°.

Two Unusual Breads

MARTHA'S BEER BREAD

Martha burst in with a plate of buttered bread. "Look what my cousin sent me!" "The bread?" "NO, silly, the recipe—it's made with beer!" So we poured fresh coffee and soon had all the bread eaten up.

3 cups self-rising flour
3 tablespoons sugar
1 12-ounce can beer

Combine the flour and sugar and stir in the beer. Spoon the dough into a well-buttered loaf pan. Bake at 375° for 45 minutes, or until the loaf sounds hollow "when the bottom of the pan is thumped."

For variation, $\frac{1}{4}$ cup wheat germ or $\frac{1}{2}$ cup raisins can be added to the dry ingredients.

UFFCULME FRUIT LOAF

At last! A fruit bread that is not too sweet—and better yet—is *full* of fruit.

$2\frac{1}{2}$ cups mixed raisins, sultanas, currants
1 cup apple cider
$1\frac{2}{3}$ cups self-rising flour
$\frac{1}{2}$ cup chopped walnuts
$\frac{2}{3}$ cup brown sugar, firmly packed
2 eggs

Place the raisins, currants, and cider in a bowl, cover, and allow to stand overnight. Mix together the flour, walnuts, and sugar. Beat the eggs and add, alternately with the fruit mixture, to the dry ingredients. Mix well. Butter a loaf pan and place a piece of parchment or oiled brown paper in the bottom. This is a MUST. Pour in the batter. Bake at 350° for 30 minutes. Reduce the oven to 325° for an additional 30 to 45 minutes, or until the loaf is golden brown and firm. Remove from the pan and cool. This is terribly good served with butter.

Scones and Quick Breads

SKILLET SCONES ↻ 2 dozen

These are excellent hot, with lots of butter, and not at all bad cold. Besides, they're one of the few breads that can be baked without an oven.

2 cups sifted flour
1 tablespoon baking powder
2 tablespoons sugar
½ teaspoon salt
½ cup raisins or currants
1 large egg
¼ cup salad oil
¼ cup cream or evaporated milk

Mix and sift the dry ingredients and then toss in raisins. Beat egg and combine with oil and milk. Dump this all at once into the dry ingredients and mix lightly with a fork.

Turn dough onto a floured board and knead 5 to 10 minutes. Pat into two circles about ½ inch thick and cut each circle into twelve wedges. Bake on an ungreased griddle or heavy frying pan 6 to 10 minutes per side, or until scones are golden brown.

NON-CRUMBLING CORN CAKES ↻ 1 dozen

⅔ cup cornmeal
½ cup unsifted flour
2 tablespoons sugar
1 teaspoon baking powder
½ teaspoon salt
¼ teaspoon baking soda
½ stick butter
⅓ cup milk
1 egg

Sift dry ingredients together and cut in butter. Beat egg with the milk and pour into the cornmeal mixture, stirring only enough to moisten. Drop from a tablespoon onto a well-greased baking sheet. The cakes will spread to about 3 inches, so allot each one sufficient space. Bake at 375° for about 15 minutes.

BIB CORNBREAD

Unlike the preceding corn cakes, this bread tends to crumble down the shirtfront of the unwary. A nice excuse for using plenty of butter, maple syrup, or honey.

1 *cup yellow cornmeal*
1 *tablespoon sugar*
½ *teaspoon salt*
2 *tablespoons flour*
2 *tablespoons shortening*
1 *cup boiling water*
2 *large eggs*

Combine dry ingredients. Stir in the boiling water and shortening, mixing well and adding a little more water if it seems too dry. Set aside to cool, while separating the eggs and beating the yolks until lemony and the whites quite stiff. Now stir yolks into the cornmeal mixture, then fold in the whites. Pour into a well-greased 8-inch-square pan and bake 20 to 25 minutes at 400°.

IRISH SODA BREAD

To be eaten hot or cold, this is one quick bread that is good for sandwiches.

4 *cups flour*
2½ *teaspoons salt*
1 *teaspoon baking soda*
⅓ *cup sugar*
1 *tablespoon caraway seeds*
½ *cup currants*
½ *cup raisins*
2 *cups buttermilk*
1 *egg*

Combine all ingredients and work on a board with an additional ¾ cup flour. Shape into a round loaf, slash a cross on the top, place on a greased baking sheet, and bake for about 45 minutes at 350°. Thump the loaf on its bottom. If it sounds hollow, it's done.

Lazy Irish Bread can be made by adding a tablespoon each of shortening and sugar along with currants and caraway seeds to biscuit mix and milk. Then proceed as above.

IRISH BROWN BREAD

4⅓ *cups sifted flour*
3 *teaspoons baking soda*
1 *teaspoon sugar*
2 *teaspoons salt*
1⅔ *cups crushed all-bran*
2½ *cups buttermilk*

Sift dry ingredients and combine with crushed all-bran. Pour in buttermilk and stir just enough to moisten. Press dough into well-greased bread pan (9 x 5 x 3) and bake at 350° for 1 hour.

A handful of currants and a tablespoon of caraway seeds mixed with the dry ingredients is a pleasant variation. To some it is a necessity.

PUMPKIN BREAD

This is best cold with some butter or cream cheese.

2½ *cups sifted flour*
1 *tablespoon baking powder*
1 *teaspoon salt*
2 *teaspoons cinnamon*
1 *teaspoon ground cloves*
½ *teaspoon mace*
½ *teaspoon baking soda*

1 *cup chopped walnuts*
½ *cup shortening*
1 *cup brown sugar*
2 *eggs*
1 *cup buttermilk*
¾ *cup canned pumpkin*

SCONES AND QUICK BREADS

Sift together flour, baking powder, salt, spices, and soda. Mix in the walnuts. Cream shortening and sugar until light and fluffy, add eggs, and beat well. Combine buttermilk and pumpkin and add to the creamed mixture alternately with flour mixture. Turn batter into a well-greased 5½ × 9½-inch loaf pan. Bake at 350° for 1 hour and 15 minutes. Turn out of pan and cool on a rack.

V. I. P. COFFEE CAKE

This coffee cake is not frugal. It should be all eaten up while it is hot, for any remaining until the next day has the texture of a ponderous pound cake.

½ *pound butter*
1¼ *cups sugar*
2 *eggs*
1 *cup sour cream*
2 *cups flour*
½ *teaspoon soda*
1½ *teaspoons baking powder*
1 *teaspoon vanilla*

¾ *cup finely chopped walnuts*
1 *teaspoon cinnamon*
2 *tablespoons sugar*

Beat together the butter, sugar, and eggs until light and fluffy. Blend in the sour cream. Sift and measure flour and resift with dry ingredients. Add to the cream mixture and vanilla and blend gently but well.

Pour half the batter into a well-buttered and floured 9-inch tube pan. Sprinkle on half the walnut-cinnamon-sugar mixture. Pour in the remaining batter and top with remaining walnut mixture. Place in a cold oven, set to 350°, and bake for 55 minutes. It will serve eight to ten.

WHOLEMEAL BISCUITS   3 dozen

These are English, not American, biscuits. Serve them with Cheddar cheese for lunch or with jam or honey as a dessert. A tin of Wholemeal Biscuits is a welcome addition to the Poor Poet's work space.

2½ cups graham flour
1 teaspoon soda
½ teaspoon cream of tartar
¼ teaspoon baking powder
¼ teaspoon salt
¼ cup sugar or honey
½ stick butter
buttermilk (about ½ cup)

Sift together the dry ingredients and rub the butter in with the fingertips. Add buttermilk and mix to a soft dough. Shape into small balls about an inch apart on a buttered baking sheet. Flatten each ball by pressing firmly with the bottom of a glass. (Dip the glass in flour so it will not stick.) Bake the biscuits at 400° for 25 to 30 minutes. Turn off oven, allow it to cool slightly, but leave the biscuits in so that they become thoroughly dry.

SALTED BISCUITS

Again, English, not American, biscuits. Use as a base for sandwich spreads or simply eat them as they are.

2 cups flour
1 teaspoon salt
¼ teaspoon pepper
pinch of cayenne
2 tablespoons butter
1 cup grated dry cheese
cold water

Sift the dry ingredients and work the butter into this. Stir in cheese. Add sufficient water to make a stiff dough and mix carefully with a fork. Roll out very thinly on a floured board and cut into rounds or squares or rectangles. Prick each biscuit with a fork. Bake on a buttered baking sheet at 350° for 7 to 10 minutes.

Crackers

SCOTCH WHEAT THINS   ც 8 dozen

1½ cups graham flour
½ cup white flour
½ teaspoon salt
⅓ cup butter
1 tablespoon honey
⅓ cup boiling water

Cut butter into dry ingredients. Add honey and boiling water and mix well. (Throughout, hands work better than a fork or spoon.) Chill dough, roll *thin*, cut in squares or what have you, and bake 12 to 15 minutes at 325° or until crackers are crisp and light brown.

TAJ MAHAL FLATBREAD   ც 2 dozen

This bread is necessary for a curry dinner, and also good with soup or salad.

1½ cups flour
1 teaspoon turmeric
¼ teaspoon salt
½ teaspoon soda
½ teaspoon coarsely ground pepper
½ stick butter
  water

Sift dry ingredients and blend in pepper and butter. Add only enough water to make a stiff dough. Pinch out marble-size balls and roll on a floured board to 4-inch rounds. Bake on an ungreased cookie sheet at 400° for 3 minutes. Turn with a spatula and bake on the other side for the same amount of time.

If an oven isn't available, the flatbread can be baked on a heavy griddle or skillet.

COWBOY BREAD ↻ 1 dozen

Not recommended for weight-watchers, Cowboy Bread is excellent with chili beans, highly seasoned stews, or big combination salads.

2 cups flour ($\frac{1}{2}$ whole wheat flour is good)
4 teaspoons baking powder
1 teaspoon salt
$\frac{1}{2}$ cup water
fat for semi-deep frying

Combine dry ingredients. Add water gradually with one hand while working the mixture into a soft dough with the other. More water may be necessary, depending on the barometer reading. Form the dough into two or three balls. Flour hands and clap dough out to a pancake about 6 to 8 inches in diameter. Drop into hot fat and fry quickly until it is crisp and brown on both sides. Drain and serve while still hot.

SCOTCH OATCAKES ↻ 8

1 cup sifted flour
1 tablespoon sugar
1 teaspoon baking powder
$\frac{1}{2}$ teaspoon salt

1$\frac{3}{4}$ cups rolled oats
$\frac{1}{4}$ cup wheat germ
$\frac{1}{3}$ cup shortening
$\frac{1}{2}$ cup milk

Sift flour, sugar, baking powder, and salt. Relying again on hands, not spoons, blend in oatmeal, wheat germ, and shortening. (Butter-lovers or those not too short of funds might prefer to use some or all butter here.) Pour in milk and mix until sticky. Do this also with the hands; it's easier and, besides, oatmeal and milk are great for the skin. Divide dough into eight balls and roll fairly thin on a floured board. Cut each round part way through into wedges. Bake at 375° for 15 to 20 minutes or until crisp and light brown.

A Yeast Bread for Busy Poets

Most yeast breads result in a floury kitchen and considerable time consumed. A large bowl of rising dough is a bed adored by kittens. Contrarily, this yeast bread requires only one bowl and a baking pan. It requires very little watching. And a cardboard carton turned over the rising dough will foil the most charming kitten.

1 *pound whole wheat flour*
1 *package dry yeast*
1 *tablespoon sugar*
1 *teaspoon salt*
warm water

Mix flour, salt, and sugar in a large bowl and make a well in the center. Into this pour the yeast that has been dissolved in about 2 tablespoons of warm water. Then add 1½ cups warm water and stir well with the best wooden spoon. The mixture should be soft and sticky. Pour the dough into a *well*-greased bread pan, cover with a cloth, and set in a warm place to rise for about 20 minutes. The dough should come just to the top of the pan. Bake at 425° for approximately 1 hour. A good test for doneness is to thump the bottom of the loaf; it should sound hollow.

This is a heavy, moist loaf, and those with more delicate tastes might prefer using half white flour.

Breadloaves

One nice use for bread is sandwiches. Fail to be limited to the usual and ponder the breadloaf.

Almost anything that is good between two slices of

bread is better in a breadloaf. Except peanut butter, perhaps.

The loaf itself, scooped out, makes a dish. It is filled with a combination of ingredients and the bottom crust is refitted as a lid. Wrapped in foil or brown paper, the whole is either baked or well chilled; and when it comes to the table is devoured—dish and all.

French bread, a milk loaf, or almost any bread with a crisp crust can be used. Whatever the choice, the loaf must be unsliced. And however the bread is stuffed it is first prepared as follows: turn the loaf upside down and cut through the bottom crust, leaving about an inch around the edges. Remove the crust in one piece and scoop out the inside. Allow the inside of the shell to dry a little so that the filling will not soak through.

Breadloaves are superior for picnics and covered dish dinners. For, still encased in their foil coats, they are bundled in several layers of newspaper, and will stay either hot or cold for hours. Then, at the end of the day, there's no plate to retrieve, no dirty dish to wash.

Each breadloaf will serve four to six generously.

EAST SIDER

1 *loaf dark rye bread*
1 *pint cottage cheese*
½ *pint sour cream*
 butter

Scoop out the loaf and generously butter the inside. Mix cottage cheese and sour cream with the crumbs that have been taken out of the loaf. Stuff and replace lid. Wrap in foil and refrigerate for an hour or two.

SEPTEMBER SPECIAL

1 *round loaf French bread*
butter
1½ *to 2 cups grated zucchini*
1 *cup grated Jack or Cheddar cheese*
¼ *pound mushrooms, sliced*
½ *cup yogurt*
12 *cherry tomatoes, halved*
1 *4-ounce can chopped ripe olives*
½ *tablespoon basil*
salt and pepper
alfalfa sprouts

Scoop out the loaf and butter the inside.

Toss together gently all ingredients except the alfalfa sprouts. Fill the loaf, alternating a layer of the vegetable-cheese mixture with a handful of sprouts. Wrap the breadloaf in foil and refrigerate for an hour or two, or better—serve it then and there.

BREADLOAF BEANS

1 *round loaf French bread*
2 *one-pound cans baked beans (or chili beans, etc.)*
butter

Scoop out the loaf and butter the insides. Heat the beans and drain off as much of the liquid as possible. Stuff the loaf with the beans and a handful of crumbs. Replace cover, wrap in brown paper, and bake for 15 minutes at 425°.

A PICNIC LOAF

1 *round loaf French bread*
4 *tomatoes*
1 *bunch green onions*
1 *3-ounce can chopped ripe olives*
1 *3-ounce jar pimiento-stuffed olives*
2 *tablespoons capers*
2 *tablespoons paprika*
  salt and pepper
  olive oil

Scoop out the loaf and smear the inside with 3 or 4 tablespoons olive oil. Chop the tomatoes and onions. Drain and slice the pimiento-stuffed olives. Combine all the ingredients with enough crumbs to fill the loaf. Replace the lid, wrap in foil, and store in the refrigerator overnight. Wrap the loaf and a chilled bottle of good white wine in several layers of newspaper and be off to the woods.

BREADLOAF BARBECUE

1 *round loaf French or milk bread*
1½ *pounds ground beef*
½ *cup bread crumbs*
½ *cup chili sauce*
1 *teaspoon Worcestershire sauce*
1 *teaspoon vinegar*
1 *teaspoon chili powder*
1 *tablespoon horseradish*
¼ *cup chopped onions*
1 *clove garlic*
1 *teaspoon salt*
  pepper
  fat or oil

Scoop out the loaf and set aside. Combine all the other ingredients. Brown in some hot fat, stirring so that the mixture is crumbly. Drain excess fat from time to time. When the meat is almost done drain fat finally and well and stuff the meat into the loaf. Wrap in brown paper and bake 15 minutes at 425°.

SUNDAY-IN-THE-PARK LOAF

Chicken is for Sunday, so here's a breadloaf to fit the weather. Plan for a sunny day, and a cold loaf. But if a cool breeze is forecast, dash the loaf into the oven and pack along a steaming repast.

1 round loaf French bread
2 cups diced cooked chicken
1 cup dry white wine
1 cup coarsely chopped walnuts
1 cup diced celery
¼ cup chopped pimiento
2 tablespoons chopped onions
3 tablespoons chopped parsley
½ cup mayonnaise
½ cup sour cream or yogurt
1 teaspoon lemon juice
2 dashes Tabasco
salt and pepper
butter

Marinate the chicken in wine for several hours and drain well. Mix with all the remaining ingredients.

For a hot day: Scoop out and butter the loaf and stuff with the chicken mixture and perhaps a handful of cherry tomatoes and pitted ripe olives. Replace the lid, wrap the loaf in foil, and chill well.

If a cloud comes over: Heat the chicken mixture in the top part of a double boiler and stuff into a well-buttered loaf. Replace lid, wrap in brown paper, and bake for 15 to 20 minutes at 425°.

OYSTER LOAF

San Franciscans claim this dish as their own. Natives of New Orleans defend their right to ownership. Where-ever the origin, the *why* remains the same: errant husbands would buy small oyster loaves, hurry them home to their wives who would be so delighted with the treat they would fail to scold.

Poor Poets who wander might take note.

1 *round loaf milk bread*	*butter*
2 *dozen medium oysters*	*salt and pepper*
2 *eggs*	2 *or* 3 *lemons*
cracker crumbs	

Oysters must not be overcooked, so line up everything and plan to work fast.

Scoop out and butter the loaf. It can sit in the oven while the oysters are frying. Melt lots of butter in a heavy pan. Beat the eggs, and set next to them a bowl of cracker crumbs. Dip each oyster into the egg, then the crumbs, and fry quickly to a rich brown. As the oysters are done, place them in the loaf. Sprinkle with salt and pepper, replace lid, and wrap the loaf in brown paper. Bake in a hot oven (425°) for 15 minutes. Serve immediately with lemon wedges, a green salad, and white wine.

DESSERTS

Many *always* end a meal with dessert. Others would *never* think of such a thing, more often announcing this with the implication that the former are a boorish lot. (There are also those who eat desserts all the time and very little else, but they don't count.)

The Poor Poet may be cognizant of the fact that the bit of honey or sugar that is part of his dessert is also quick energy for creating, composing, constructing.

Desserts are especially necessary to save an end-of-the-month-type meal. They can be elegant though minuscule: two or three preserved figs and a spoonful of yogurt offered on a doll's plate. They can be simple though enormous, served in soup bowls to celebrate spring: warm homemade shortcake, split and buttered, filled and topped with all the first strawberries the bowl will contain, and honestly running over with whipped cream.

Fruits—In Season and Out

A tray of fresh fruits in summer or a bowl of dried fruits and nuts in winter, with a few leaves or stray flowers tucked in, is centerpiece now—dessert later.

(A similar still life, only smaller, belongs on the writer's desk, near the painter's easel, or close at hand, no matter what the craft.) Then, too, there are desserts to compound from fruits and assorted additives.

APPLES DEMIJOHN ↣ 6

6 *cooking apples*
¾ *cup sugar*
1 *cup sweet white wine*
6 *tablespoons apricot jam*
1 *or 2 jiggers brandy*

Core the apples and place in a buttered baking dish. Simmer sugar and wine together for 5 minutes; pour over apples. Cover and bake for 30 to 40 minutes in a 400° oven, or until apples are tender. Drain the syrup from the apples and thicken with the jam and brandy. Pour the syrup over the apples and serve either warm or chilled, plain or with cream.

APPLES IN BOURBON ↣ 4

A chameleon-sort of dish, Apples in Bourbon is good as an accompaniment to ham or turkey; done in a chafing dish and served plain or with vanilla ice cream, it becomes dessert. And anything that is left over can be used next morning to top a bowl of hot oatmeal.

4 *cooking apples*
6 *tablespoons sugar*
  strips of rind and juice from ½ *lemon*
1 *inch stick cinnamon*
½ *cup bourbon*

Peel and core the apples, leaving them whole or cutting into thick slices. Combine the other ingredients and bring to a boil. Care and a low flame are necessary at this point or else the syrup will burn or ignite, or both. Place the apples in the syrup, cover, and let simmer for 15 to 30 minutes, or until the apples are just tender.

RUMRUNNER BANANAS ⋈ 4

This, too, can be dessert or meat accompaniment.

4 *not-too-ripe bananas*
2 *tablespoons butter*
4 *tablespoons brown sugar*
cinnamon
¼ *cup rum*

Melt butter in a frying pan or chafing dish and place in it bananas that have been peeled and sliced in half lengthwise. Sprinkle the bananas with half the brown sugar and a dash of cinnamon and fry until they are lightly browned. Turn and repeat the process. When the bananas are just soft, pour over the rum, ignite, and serve on the spot.

WINEMAKER FIGS ⋈ 4

½ *pound dried figs*
¼ *cup chopped toasted almonds*
1 *tablespoon honey*
½ *cup port or claret*
1 *teaspoon lemon juice*

Plump the figs by steaming them in a strainer over boiling water. Mix the honey and nuts and stuff each fig. Place figs in a shallow baking dish, pour over the wine and lemon juice, and heat thoroughly in a 350° oven, basting occasionally.

Or heat the wine and lemon juice in a chafing dish, add figs, cover and cook about 10 minutes. In either case, serve hot with whipped cream flavored with a drop of almond extract.

SKEWERED FRUIT

The Poor Poet who perseveres might locate bamboo skewers that have little caps at the top, each one containing a fortune. Thread each skewer with the following:

mandarin orange sections
canned lichees
fresh or preserved
   kumquats
crystallized ginger
preserved watermelon rind
pineapple chunks

Accompany the Skewered Fruit with a basket of Soy Toasted Seeds and Nuts (see page 204).

PLUGGED MELON   6–8

1 *large honeydew, cantaloupe, or casaba*
1 *to* 1½ *cups Madeira or white dessert wine*

Cut a circular plug from the stem end of the melon and scoop out the seeds. Fill the melon with wine, replace the plug, and seal with butter or masking tape. Chill the melon for at least 2 hours (overnight is better). Serve spoonfuls of fruit with the wine ladled over.

Or—when the melon is seeded, scoop out the pulp and mix with any fresh fruits at hand. Stuff the melon and proceed as above.

And, in either case, consider the possibilities of Plugged Melon for a late breakfast or a picnic in the park.

ORANGES WITH BROWN SUGAR AND RUM   ℘ 6

4 *large oranges*   ½ *cup rum*
¼ *cup brown sugar*   *orange flower water*

    Peel and slice the oranges and allow to chill well. In the meantime, chop the peel and place in a saucepan with the sugar, rum to cover, and any juice from peeling fruit. Heat the sauce to simmer, turn off heat, and allow to stand for at least 2 hours, covered. About an hour before serving, strain the syrup over the oranges, add a dash or two of orange flower water, and stir once. Present in goblets or white porcelain bowls.

CARAMEL PEACHES   ℘ 6

6 *peaches*   1 *cup brown sugar*
1 *tablespoon butter*   ¼ *cup cream*
                            nutmeg

    Peel the peaches, leave whole, and place in a heavy frying pan in which butter is melting. Sprinkle sugar over the fruit and simmer, uncovered, for 30 minutes. Turn and baste the peaches every so often. Just before serving, pour cream over and bring just to a boil. Grate a little nutmeg over each serving.

SNOWBOUND PEACHES   ℘ 4

8 *canned peach halves*   ½ *cup currant jelly*
1 *tablespoon cornstarch*   1 *tablespoon lemon juice*
⅓ *cup sugar*   1 *tablespoon butter*
  dash of salt   ¼ *teaspoon cinnamon*
½ *cup Burgundy*   ⅓ *cup shredded coconut*
½ *cup syrup from peaches*

    Place drained peaches, cut side up, in a buttered baking dish. Combine the cornstarch, sugar, and salt in a saucepan; add the wine and peach syrup. Stir until smooth and then add the jelly. Bring slowly to a boil, stirring constantly. Continue cooking and stirring until the sauce is thickened and clear—2 or 3 minutes. Remove from heat; add lemon juice, butter, and cinnamon. Pour the sauce over the peaches and sprinkle with coconut.

Bake for 30 minutes at 350° and serve warm to snowbound poets.

CRANBERRY PEARS   ↩ 3–6

6 *pears*
1 *can strained cranberry sauce*
½ *can water*
2 *jiggers brandy*
   thick cream

Peel, halve, and core the pears. Melt the cranberry sauce and water over low heat and simmer the pears in this syrup until they are just tender. When cool, stir in the brandy, but don't stir so violently that the pears are broken. Serve with thick cream to three or four.

Cranberry Pears, without the cream, is a fine accompaniment to roast turkey or pork. In this case, six may be served.

AMBROSIA

True ambrosia is not dressed up with marshmallows or maraschino cherries or like trappings. It is clean, sharp, and pure, and so desired by Poor Poets—others, too.

Make Ambrosia by cutting up equal parts of oranges and pineapple (preferably fresh), sprinkled with a little sugar and a handful of grated coconut (also preferably fresh). Cover and let chill overnight.

This is excellent as dessert after a big Christmas dinner.

KOSCHAFF

1 *pound dried prunes*
1 *pound dried figs*
½ *pound dried apricots*
½ *pound raisins*
¼ *pound blanched almonds or pine nuts*
1 *or* 2 *lemons*

Soak the prunes overnight, then simmer with the lemons that have been sliced paper-thin. When the prunes are almost tender add the remaining fruits and nuts, remove from the fire, cover, and let chill for at least another day. Serve as is or with a bowl of yogurt on the side.

Koschaff keeps for days and days in the refrigerator.

Cookies

These are the reasons for baking cookies: It is fun. It makes the kitchen smell good. It results in a tin of little desserts. It gives time for contemplation—and an excuse for pinching a sample from each pan.

Even the Poor Poet with only a hot plate for stove can make cookies, though his repertoire may be limited.

HOT PLATE CURRANT BARS ~ 4 dozen

2 *cups sifted cake flour*
1 *teaspoon baking powder*
¼ *teaspoon salt*
1½ *cups sugar*
3 *tablespoons butter*
1 *teaspoon grated lemon rind*
¾ *cup currants*
1 *egg*
milk

Sift the flour with the other dry ingredients and cut in the butter. Add lemon rind, currants, the egg slightly beaten, and a splash of milk. The dough must be on the dry side, yet held together. Plunk the dough onto a floured board and roll quite thin. (A wine bottle works fine here.) Now cut small bars, diamonds, or fancier shapes. Bake slowly on a buttered griddle, browning each side neatly.

SKILLET OATCAKES ༧ 2 dozen

Appended to this recipe, and in a fine Spencerian hand, was the notation: "These cakes will not absorb any fat, are very nice and not pernicious." What the writer failed to add was that care must be taken in frying, for the cakes will spread out amazingly and the thin edges must be cautiously pushed toward the middle.

3 tablespoons each granulated and brown sugar
1 teaspoon butter
3 teaspoons water
2 tablespoons rolled oats
⅓ cup finely chopped nut meats
½ teaspoon cinnamon
2½ tablespoons flour
  butter for frying

Cream sugar and butter, then stir in the remaining ingredients, one by one, and in the order given. Drop by skimpy teaspoonfuls onto a well-buttered griddle and fry slowly until caramelized and brown on one side; turn and brown the other. Cool on waxed paper.

POET WAFERS ༧ 3 dozen

3 eggs
½ cup sugar
½ teaspoon vanilla
½ cup water
½ cup melted butter
1 cup flour

Beat eggs and sugar well, blend in vanilla and water, and the melted butter and flour alternately. Butter a griddle and bake the cookies one at a time (use a tablespoon of batter for each) for about 1½ minutes on each side. Roll cookies around the handle of a wooden spoon while they're still warm. These may be eaten as they are or filled with whipped cream.

RUM BALLS ↻ 3½–4 dozen

These don't call for any sort of stove at all—just patience.

3 cups crushed vanilla wafers (¼-pound package)
1 cup confectioners' sugar
3 tablespoons powdered cocoa
1 cup finely chopped walnuts or pecans
3 tablespoons corn syrup
¼ to ½ cup rum

Dump all the ingredients into a bowl and, using hands, mix well. Pinch out small pieces and roll into balls. Roll these in additional confectioners' sugar, pack in a jar with a good tight lid, and allow to age for several weeks, at least.

When the Poor Poet has a kitchen with an oven and a breadboard and a rolling pin he is very lucky indeed. For then, when the muse won't come and the paper in the typewriter is as pristine as an hour ago, it is perhaps time to make cookies. Especially the rolled and cut kind. There is a therapeutic something about rolling the dough, cutting designs, and contemplating the view while waiting for each batch to bake . . . and, perchance, the muse to return.

CARDAMOM COOKIES   8 dozen

The bon vivant of Scandinavia chews cardamom seeds as a breath sweetener. Ground and made into cookies, the seeds loose a share of their cleansing effect. However, these cookies are exceedingly refreshing, as well as quite crisp.

⅓ cup shortening
1 cup sugar
1 egg
¼ cup milk
2 teaspoons lemon juice
1 tablespoon grated lemon rind

2 cups sifted flour
2 teaspoons baking powder
½ teaspoon salt
1½ teaspoons ground cardamom

Beat together the shortening, sugar, and egg. Add milk, lemon juice, and rind and mix well. Sift together the dry ingredients and stir the dough thoroughly. Chill and roll a small quantity at a time on a floured board. Cut with a round cookie cutter, place on an ungreased pan, and bake for about 5 minutes at 400°.

ANISE RUSKS   3 dozen

2 large eggs
½ cup plus 2 tablespoons sugar
1¼ cups flour
1 tablespoon anise seeds
1 teaspoon olive oil

Beat the eggs and sugar for 10 minutes. Sift flour and blend thoroughly (gently, though) into the egg-sugar mixture. Stir in anise seeds and oil. Pour into a well-buttered and floured 8-inch-square pan. Bake at 375° for 20 minutes or until the cake is done.

Turn cake out of pan and slice in half and then crosswise in ½-inch slices. Place slices on a well-buttered cookie sheet and return them to the oven. Allow to brown on one side for about 5 minutes, then turn and brown on the other.

Stored in an air-tight tin, Anise Rusks keep for a week or two.

POPPY SEED COOKIES   ც 8 dozen

4 *eggs*
1 *cup sugar*
½ *cup salad oil*
1 *tablespoon grated lemon rind*
1 *tablespoon lemon juice*
1 *teaspoon vanilla*
¼ *cup poppy seeds*
4½ *cups flour*
1½ *teaspoons baking powder*
½ *teaspoon salt*
cinnamon

Beat the eggs well, then slowly beat in the next six ingredients. Sift 2 cups flour with the other dry ingredients and add to the batter. Now stir in enough additional flour to make a stiff dough. Roll thin on a floured board, cut, sprinkle with a little sugar and cinnamon, and bake at 350° for about 8 minutes.

PFEFFERNÜSSE   ც 3½ dozen

A good Christmas tradition not to be overlooked by Poor Poets.

2¼ *cups flour*
½ *teaspoon each cloves, nutmeg, and cinnamon*
¼ *teaspoon each ginger, black pepper, cardamom, and baking soda*
2 *eggs*
1 *cup dark brown sugar, firmly packed*
⅓ *cup finely chopped walnuts*

Beat eggs and sugar for 5 minutes. Sift together and add the dry ingredients. Stir in the chopped nuts. Roll cookies the size of large marbles in wet hands. Bake on a greased cookie sheet for 12 to 15 minutes at 375°.

Now, when all the Pfeffernüsse are baked, whip up the following glaze:

½ cup water
1½ cups sugar
  dash cream of tartar
1 egg white

Boil the water, sugar, and cream of tartar to 235° and pour over the stiffly beaten egg white—beating wildly at the same time. Drop the Pfeffernüsse into the glaze, stir to coat, and then remove to a rack to dry.

MORAVIAN COOKIES ↆ 8 dozen

These are good at Christmas, or any time when the weather is brisk.

¼ cup butter
½ cup molasses
3 tablespoons brown sugar, packed
  a scant ½ teaspoon each ginger, cloves, and cinnamon
⅛ teaspoon each nutmeg and allspice
  a dash each salt and black pepper
  a scant ½ teaspoon soda
1⅞ cups sifted cake flour

Heat the molasses and stir in the butter. Add sugar, spices, and soda. Stir in the flour and beat well. Cover the dough and let it stand in a cool place for a week or more. Roll the dough paper-thin, cut, and bake at 375° for about 6 minutes.

ANISPLATZCHEN   ~ 7 dozen

When the gods are with the Poor Poet his Anisplatzchen will turn out like little mushroom caps: a crisp bottom, a bit of air space, and a meringue on top. Much depends on the temperature of the eggs, the length of beating (Grandmother said at least an hour and a half with a big wooden spoon), and the barometer reading.

3 *eggs*
1 *cup plus* 1 *tablespoon sugar*
1¾ *cups sifted flour*
¾ *teaspoon baking powder*
½ *teaspoon salt*
1½ *tablespoons anise seeds*

The eggs must be at room temperature or a little better. Using an electric mixer, beat them for 10 minutes. Add sugar gradually, beating constantly, and continue for another half hour. Now add the sifted dry ingredients and anise and beat for an additional 5 minutes. Drop heaping teaspoonfuls of batter well apart on a buttered and floured tin. Let the batter dry for 12 hours. Bake for about 10 minutes at 325° or until the cakes have puffed and the bottoms are golden. Store in air-tight tins.

LECKERLEIN   ~ 12 dozen plus

These are definitely *not* for the impatient taste-tester. For the dough is made one day, stored in a crock, and all but forgotten for six months to a year. Then, another day is chosen and the cookies are baked and frosted. Now they are stacked into a tin between layers of waxed paper and topped with a cloth generously drenched with rum. The tin is sealed and hidden away for a year— perhaps two. Once in a while the seal is broken and more rum is added, and at these times it is permissible to taste.

Poor Poets who developed a passion for Leckerlein are advised to set up an annual routine so that once the cycle is begun they must never again have to wait 24 long months for the heady flavor of this exceptional cake.

3 pounds honey
½ cup butter
½ pound almonds
¼ pound citron
2 cups sugar
2 teaspoons each allspice, cinnamon, cloves, mace, and nutmeg
1 tablespoon grated lemon rind
plenty of flour
½ ounce carbonate of powdered ammonia
½ cup rum

Heat the honey and melt the butter in it. Stir in the almonds that have been blanched and chopped fine, and chopped citron, and the sugar. Now add the spices and lemon rind. Sift flour and begin stirring it in, adding and stirring until the dough is so stiff that there is some difficulty getting the spoon through it. Dissolve the carbonate of ammonia (available from a druggist) in rum and finally stir this into the dough. Cover and store for at least 6 months.

When baking time arrives, pat the dough into well-greased pans to about ¼ inch thick and bake at 350°. Cut the cake into squares and ice with confectioners' sugar that has been melted with a little water and lemon juice in the top part of a double boiler. Store the cookies as directed above and wait . . .

Desserts from Another Time and Place

As a gala ending to a gala feast, fancy a cluster of desserts that Grandmother considered everyday fare.

For some not too clear reason—packaged foods, perhaps—the wonderful desserts have all but disappeared from the table. The Poor Poet, however, should consider them not as an extravagance (although they really are) but rather as an exercise in true creativity.

PANETTONE ✌ 8–10

The Guardian reported, "After a brief struggle with two bank clerks at Swindon, yesterday, three masked raiders escaped in a car with several bags belonging to the clerks." Following a description of both raid and escape, the story concluded, "The bags they stole contained the clerks' lunch."

It is hoped, for the sake of the raiders, that at least one lunch bag contained a generous slab of Panettone. It's a cake that keeps well and could be expected to survive a bank robbery.

½ cup shortening
½ cup butter
1 cup sugar
2 teaspoons almond flavoring
1 teaspoon rum flavoring or vanilla
3 eggs

3 cups flour
3 teaspoons baking powder
½ teaspoon salt
1¼ cups milk
½ cup each chopped walnuts, raisins, and glacéd fruit

Cream together the butter, shortening, and sugar. Add the almond and rum flavorings. Beat the eggs well and then beat them into the creamed mixture. Sift together the dry ingredients and blend them alternately with the milk into the creamed mixture. Last, fold in the nuts and fruits.

Pour into a greased and floured angel food cake pan and bake at 350° for 1½ hours, then reduce the heat to 250° and bake an additional 15 minutes. Turn the cake out onto a rack to cool.

BREAD PUDDING   ❦ 6

> 3 *slices toast*
> ½ *cup raisins*
> ½ *cup chopped candied fruit*
> 3 *eggs*
> ⅓ *cup sugar*
> ½ *teaspoon salt*
> 1 *teaspoon grated lemon rind*
> 1 *teaspoon vanilla*
> ¼ *teaspoon almond extract*
> 2 *cups* rich *milk*

Cube the toast and place in a buttered baking dish (about 10 × 6 × 2) and sprinkle with the fruits. Separate one egg, reserve the white, and beat the yolk with the other two eggs. Scald the milk and add it gradually to the eggs, along with the other ingredients. Keep up the beating process. Pour the egg-milk mixture over the bread and fruits, and bake at 350° for 25 minutes or until custard is set. Beat the egg white stiff, fold in 2 tablespoons sugar, and swirl on top of the pudding. Bake until the meringue is golden. Serve warm or at room temperature.

GALA DESSERTS

CASSATA   ₻ 8–10

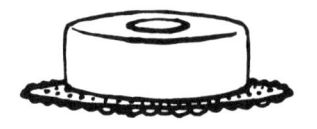

    not-too-fresh sponge cake
1 *pound Ricotta cheese*
1½ *cups sugar*
¼ *teaspoon salt*
¼ *cup grated semi-sweet chocolate*
3 *tablespoons chopped candied fruit*
3 *tablespoons rum or orange flower water*

    Slice the sponge cake an inch thick and line a spring mold. Beat all the other ingredients and pour into the mold. Top with additional slices of cake that have been crumbled. Refrigerate overnight and when ready to serve remove the cake from the mold and dust with powdered sugar and a few sliced blanched almonds, if they're available.

FLOATING ISLAND   ₻ 6–8

    There is absolutely nothing so nice on a summer day as a big crystal bowl full of Floating Island.
For the custard:

2 *cups milk*
3 *egg yolks*
½ *teaspoon vanilla*
¼ *cup sugar*
⅛ *teaspoon salt*

    Scald the milk in a double boiler. Beat the egg yolks with the sugar. Slowly add the hot milk to the yolks, stirring constantly. Return the mixture to the double boiler and continue stirring and cooking until the custard thickens and a thin coating is formed on the spoon. Add salt and vanilla and pour into a serving dish.

For the islands:

3 *egg whites*
3 *tablespoons powdered sugar*
1 *teaspoon vanilla*

Beat the whites until stiff, then gradually add the sugar and vanilla. Place by spoonfuls on hot, not boiling, water and cover. Test in a few minutes by running a knife through an island. If the knife comes out clean the islands are done. Place them on the custard and chill well.

RUMOS TORTE 8–10

¾ *cup sugar*
¾ *cup water*
¼ *cup rum*
½ *teaspoon vanilla*
3 *sponge cake layers*
¼ *cup raspberry jam*
¼ *cup ground almonds*
rum-flavored whipped cream

Combine the sugar and water and boil for 5 minutes. Add rum and vanilla and one of the sponge cake layers, crumbled. Spread half the jam on the second sponge cake layer and top with the rum-soaked crumbs, the almonds, and the third sponge cake layer which has also been spread with jam. The jam side goes down, this time. Weight the cake with a flat plate and let stand overnight. Serve doused with whipped cream that has been generously spiked with additional rum.

CHEESE CAKE 8–10

The cheese cake fancier, haunted by repeated failure, might be put in better mental state to know that there is at least *one* foolproof formula.

graham cracker crumb crust for an 8-inch pan
½ *pound cream cheese*
1 *large egg*
6 *tablespoons sugar*
½ *teaspoon grated lemon rind*
1 *teaspoon orange flower water*
½ *cup sour cream*
1 *tablespoon sugar*
a few drops vanilla
salt

Cream together the cream cheese, egg, 6 tablespoons sugar, lemon rind, orange flower water, and a dash of salt, and pour the mixture into an 8-inch pie pan lined with graham cracker crust. Top this with the sour cream that has been mixed with a tablespoon of sugar and the vanilla. Bake in a 350° oven for 8 minutes. Cool, and chill before serving. This is quite rich and goes a long, long way.

FRIED CREAM ℧ 12

3 *egg yolks*   1 *inch vanilla bean*
1 *jigger rum*   *grating of nutmeg*
¼ *cup sugar*   *cracker crumbs*
  pinch salt   1 *egg*
3 *tablespoons cornstarch* *butter*
2 *cups cream*   ¼ *cup rum*

Beat together the egg yolks, jigger of rum, sugar, and salt. Make a paste of the cornstarch and an equal part of water or milk and add to the egg yolk mixture. Heat the cream with the vanilla bean and nutmeg and gradually stir this into the yolks. Cook and stir in a double boiler until the custard is quite thick and smooth. Remove the vanilla bean, rinse it, and save it for another day. Pour the cream into a buttered shallow pan and chill.

When ready to serve, cut the cream into small rectangles and dip in crumbs, then in a slightly beaten egg, and once again in crumbs. Fry in butter or hot deep fat, place on a warm serving plate, slosh with ¼ cup warm rum, and ignite.

A rich dessert that calls for tiny cups of strong Italian coffee.

WHISKEY PUDDING   ℘ 12

This is almost too elegant.

½ *pound lady fingers*
½ *cup ground almonds*
¼ *cup sliced maraschino cherries*
8 *eggs*
2 *cups bourbon*
¾ *cup sugar*
  dash of almond or vanilla extract
  salt

Line a large serving dish (crystal is preferred) with split lady fingers and cherries and sprinkle in half the almonds. Separate the eggs and beat the yolks with two tablespoons sugar until they are light. Warm the bourbon in the top of a double boiler and carefully stir it into the yolks. Cook the custard over hot water until it is quite thick, then pour it into the lady-finger-lined dish.

Beat the egg whites until stiff and fold in the remaining sugar, a dash of salt, and the almond extract. Spread on top of the custard, sprinkle with the rest of the almonds, and bake in a 325° oven until the meringue is golden.

If the best crystal serving dish was used, bake the meringue on a cookie sheet and then transfer it to the custard.

Whiskey Pudding is to be served cold.

OZARK PUDDING

1 egg	⅛ teaspoon salt
¾ cup sugar	1 cup chopped apples
3 heaping tablespoons flour	½ cup chopped walnuts
	1 teaspoon vanilla
1¼ teaspoons baking powder	1 cup cream, whipped

Beat the egg and sugar until light and creamy. Sift together the dry ingredients and add to the egg mixture. Blend well. Fold in apples and nuts, and finally the vanilla. Pour into a buttered baking dish. Bake for 30 minutes at 325°. Serve warm with whipped cream.

SCRIPTURE CAKE

A recipe to be read rather than followed.

1 *cup butter*, JUDGES, 5:25
3½ *cups flour*, I. KINGS, 4:22
2 *cups sugar*, JER. 6:20
2 *cups raisins*, I. SAM. 30:12
2 *cups figs*, I. SAM. 30:12
1 *cup water*, GEN. 24:17
1 *cup almonds*, GEN. 43:11
  little salt, LEV. 2:13
6 *eggs*, IS. 10:14
  sweet spices to taste, I. KINGS, 10:2
1 *tablespoonful honey*, EX. 16:31

Follow Solomon's advice for making good boys and you will have a good cake, PROV. 23:14. Sift 2 teaspoonfuls of baking powder with flour, blanch the almonds, chop figs.

GILDING THE LILY

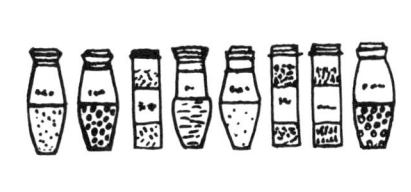

Calm anticipation of the unexpected dinner guest: a virtue of necessity for Poor Poets—and others.

A freezer stuffed with roasts, chops, stews, vegetables, soups, and pies leads to this state. So does the corner delicatessen. So, too, does a shelf of comestibles designed solely for gilding the lily.

But the gilt must be as pure and good as Mrs. March's popovers or the treats that Ratty packed into his picnic basket.

A supper of baked beans, corn bread with butter, and cole slaw, though not remarkable, is satisfying. Embellish the same menu with a tray holding many little crocks of relishes and supper becomes a feast. And—takes care of the unexpected guest.

In this category cottage cheese goes well with eggs, baked beans, or ham. It can be tossed with almost any salad. It can be folded into buttered noodles. It can be mixed with candied or dried fruits, jam or jelly, deviled meats, anchovies, or herbs for sandwiches, dips, or décor.

Sour cream or plain yogurt belongs in a big bowl next to potatoes or pilaf, peas, green beans, and eggplant. Or fruit compote.

These, along with celery, carrots, green onions, and radishes, refrigerator staples to most: to the inventive, items that not only gild the lily but recall all the treats in art and literature.

Then there are things to make and store on a shelf; insurance against the unexpected.

Relishes from Jars and Tins

MUSTARD OLIVES

¼ *cup vinegar*
1 *tablespoon dry mustard*
1 *teaspoon mustard seeds*
1 #1 *can ripe or green-ripe olives*
1 *tablespoon olive oil*

Dump mustard and mustard seeds into a small saucepan and slowly blend in the vinegar, olive oil, and liquid from the canned olives. Bring the mixture to a boil, add olives, and simmer 10 minutes. Cool and refrigerate. Mustard Olives, which should be drained just before serving, improve with several days' aging.

HERB OLIVES

1 *cup drained ripe olives*
½ *cup olive oil*
½ *bay leaf, crumbled*
1 *chili pepper, crumbled*
1 *tablespoon capers*

1 *clove garlic, mashed*
6 *rosemary leaves*
1 *teaspoon celery seeds or several leaves*

Plop everything into a jar with a good lid, shake well, and store in refrigerator for at least three days. Reshaking and taste-testing each day is permissible. When the olives have been eaten (by taste-testing?) the oil can be used for salads.

10-DAY STUFFED OLIVES

A good way to extend the life of a jar of opened and aging stuffed olives.

1 *cup stuffed green olives*
½ *teaspoon oregano*
½ *bay leaf, crumbled*
½ *teaspoon paprika*
1 *clove garlic, mashed*
¼ *cup vinegar*
¼ *cup brine from olives*

Drain the olives, reserving ¼ cup brine. Sprinkle herbs, paprika, and garlic over the olives in the jar, and then cover with vinegar and reserved brine. Cover the jar, shake, and store in the refrigerator for at least 10 days, giving the jar further shakes at intervals.

CURRIED PICKLES

⅓ *cup cider vinegar*
⅓ *cup brown sugar, firmly packed*
1 *tablespoon curry powder*
1 *12-ounce jar sliced cucumber pickles, drained*

Combine the vinegar, sugar, and curry powder and simmer for 10 minutes before pouring over the pickles and recapping the jar. Allow the concoction to stand a day or two before serving.

PRESERVED FIGS

1 *one-pound can green figs*
1 *cup tarragon vinegar*
2 *tablespoons Worcestershire*
1 *tablespoon Dijon-style mustard*
1 *tablespoon dry mustard*
½ *teaspoon cayenne*

Drain the figs and cut them in half into a glass jar. Combine the other ingredients and stir until the mustards are dissolved. Pour over the figs, cover, and let ripen in the refrigerator for at least three days.

FRUITS IN HONEY AND WINE

Canned peaches, pears, apricots, fruits for salad, or a combination, treated with honey and wine, are a superb side dish with meats or poultry.

1 *cup honey*
¾ *cup cider vinegar*
10 *whole cloves*
1 *stick cinnamon*
¼ *cup port or muscatel wine*
1½ *quarts well-drained canned fruit (2 #2½ cans)*

Combine and simmer for 5 minutes the honey, vinegar, cloves, and cinnamon. Add the wine and fruit and continue to simmer 15 minutes longer. Cool and store in refrigerator.

PICKLED BEETS

1 *#303 can sliced beets (about 2 cups)*
½ *cup juice from beets*
6 *tablespoons cider vinegar*
1 *tablespoon sugar*
1 *scant teaspoon salt*
2 *teaspoons each cloves and dry mustard*
   dash of cinnamon and allspice
1 *small clove garlic*

Pack drained beets in a quart jar. Mix the other ingredients in a saucepan, bring to a boil, and pour over the beets. Cover, cool, and refrigerate until ready to use. Good with sour cream!

Like the magic pudding, this dish can grow and grow. As the number of beet slices in the jar diminishes, whole hard-cooked eggs, sliced onions, or parboiled celery or carrot sticks can be dropped into the pickling liquid. They should be ready to eat in a day or two.

BEETS WITH HORSERADISH

1 #303 *can diced beets*
4 *tablespoons sugar*
6 *tablespoons prepared horseradish*
6 *tablespoons finely chopped onions*
4 *tablespoons vinegar*
½ *teaspoon salt*
¼ *teaspoon pepper*

Empty the drained beets into a bowl, measure in the other ingredients, stir well, cover, and refrigerate. These should be allowed to stand an hour or so before using. A must with roast beef.

PLUM SAUCE

The Chinese serve Plum Sauce as a dip for egg roll, fried shrimp, barbecued spareribs, roast pork, and roast chicken. It is not to be overlooked.

1 *cup plum jelly*
½ *cup chutney*
1 *tablespoon cider vinegar*
1 *tablespoon sugar*

Blend the four ingredients, let stand several hours, and the sauce is ready.

SAMBAL

This is a Javanese hot (!) sauce that is necessary for Nasi Goreng Rice or Rijstafel. Two-ounce jars of the imported variety are uncommon, even in specialty food shops.

4 *tablespoons raw white fish*
2 *tablespoons brown sugar*
1 *yeast cake*
1 *clove garlic*
½ *cup seeded and chopped red pepper*
½ *cup chopped onion*
½ *teaspoon salt*
¼ *cup or more peanut oil*

Chop the fish and then mix in a mortar with the yeast, garlic, and sugar until the mixture becomes a paste. Cover and let stand for 24 hours.

Grind the peppers, onion, and salt to a paste.

Pour the oil into a heavy pan with lid and fry and stir the fish paste until the fish is cooked. Stir in the vegetable paste (be sure there is sufficient oil), cover, and cook over very low heat until the oil has turned red. Makes a generous ½ cup.

DIJON MUSTARD ⌬ 2 cups

2 *cups dry white wine*
1 *cup chopped onion*
2 *cloves garlic, minced*
1 *4-ounce can dry mustard*
2 *tablespoons honey*
1 *tablespoon vegetable oil*
2 *teaspoons salt*
dash Tabasco

Simmer onion and garlic in the wine for 5 minutes. Cover and cool. Empty the mustard tin into a saucepan, and strain and add the wine mixture, beating constantly. Blend in the other ingredients, heat slowly—and don't stop stirring—until the mustard thickens. Pour into jars, cover, and keep refrigerated.

KENNETH'S ENGLISH MUSTARD ~ 2 cups

There is a side benefit to the 45 minutes of stirring: steamy mustard aromas are sure to clear the head.

1 4-*ounce can dry mustard*   6 *eggs*
1 *cup malt vinegar*   1 *cup sugar*

Stir the vinegar into the mustard in the top part of a double boiler. Cover and let stand 2 or 3 hours. Beat in the eggs one at a time—not too hard or fast! Add the sugar. Place over simmering water and stir continually for about 45 minutes or until the mustard is the consistency of mayonnaise. Pour the mustard into jars, cover, and keep refrigerated.

Vinegars

WINE VINEGAR

Vinegar, purple in color and definitely tasting like *wine*, that is sometimes found in family-style Italian restaurants may be manufactured at home. With patience. Equipment consists of an empty wine bottle with cork and a small funnel.

To proceed, pour half a cup or so of good commercial wine vinegar into the bottle. To this add (and continue adding at intervals) leftover red wines. A good wine vinegar should have developed in several months, though it will improve as time goes on. Impatient taste-testers might start several bottles at once so that at least one batch has a good year and a half to mature properly.

With luck (helped a bit by the addition of a dash or two of unprocessed apple cider) "mother" will develop in the vinegar. If it does, pour the contents of that bottle *gently* into a crock or glass jar. Cover the container with a folded dish towel, store it in a dark corner, and continue adding wine every so often.

HERB VINEGARS

Branches of fresh herbs, spirals of lemon or orange peel, chives or green onion tops, garlic cloves impaled on bamboo skewers—a wide choice for the herb vinegar maker.

Following your whim, put the branches, spirals, or skewers into clean bottles or jars. Fill with heated wine vinegar, cork or cap, and store in a dark spot for about a month.

NASTURTIUM VINEGAR

2 cups green nasturtium seeds
¼ cup salt
2 cups cider or white wine vinegar

Fill a quart jar half full of nasturtium seeds, sprinkle with salt, cover, and allow to stand overnight. Next day fill the jar with vinegar, cover with a non-corrosive lid, and let lurk in a dark cupboard to ripen for several weeks.

Seasoning Salts

Develop a customized seasoning salt (or several). It saves, for example, the effort of hauling out half a dozen jars and cartons just to make one deviled egg.

For a start, here's a seasoning salt that's good in pot roasts or stews, and with poultry.

1 *cup salt*
1 *teaspoon pepper*
1 *teaspoon paprika*
½ *teaspoon ground ginger*
½ *teaspoon dry mustard*
½ *teaspoon crushed oregano*
⅓ *teaspoon cayenne*
⅓ *teaspoon mace*
¼ *teaspoon (heaping) garlic powder*

Mix, and store in a jar with a tight lid.

Jellies

Glasses of jelly from the store, melted, treated with herbs or spices, and allowed to reset . . . a profitable kitchen adventure for a dreary day.

Melt the jelly either in the top part of a double boiler or in a small pan over a low flame. For more flavor, the herbs should be added while the jelly is hot. However, for aesthetic purposes, i.e., a branch or leaf suspended midway in the finished product, this work must be carried on while the jelly is cooling.

Apple jelly takes well to a branch of sweet basil, sage, or mint; leaves of lemon verbena, rose geranium, or nasturtium; a cinnamon stick, or several whole cloves.

Lemon jelly is picked up with the addition of a branch of tarragon, marjoram, rosemary, sage, or thyme.

Grape jelly becomes special when a broken cinnamon stick, several whole cloves, or bruised cardamom seeds are added.

And then there is:

WINE JELLY

    1 *package raspberry-flavored gelatin*
    ¾ *cup boiling water*
    ¾ *cup sherry*
    1 *tablespoon claret*
    2 *tablespoons brandy*

Dissolve the gelatin in boiling water and stir in the wines and brandy. Pour into a mold and chill until set.

Yogurt

Because yogurt is a main dish, a side dish, or an ingredient for so many recipes, the Poor Poet would do well to learn to make his own.

Bring 1 quart of milk (whole, skim, canned, or reconstituted dry) just to a boil. Cool to lukewarm and stir in 1 tablespoon commercial yogurt. Cover the container and let stand in a warm place overnight, then chill before using.

Yogurt, mixed half and half with cold water, is a good pick-me-up.

Yogurt, drained overnight or for several days in a cheesecloth-lined colander, may be turned out on a plate, sprinkled with salt, and drenched with olive oil, and used for a spread for crackers or toast. This may be varied with a sprinkling of chopped mint leaves or chopped ripe olives.

POOR POET TRIFLES

Simmer tiny beets in orange juice and serve with their uncooked tops, egg yolk balls, and shredded carrot and onion.

The milk bath was promoted as a publicity stunt. Drinking it proves more beneficial.

Spread toast with butter mixed with toasted sesame seeds and brown under a flame.

Poor Poets—and others—who combine the cocktail hour with cooking should take care that they don't overseason the food.

Sprinkle hot baked apples or pears with grated cheese.

Olives will keep for months if about an inch of olive oil is poured over the olives and their brine and the jar tightly capped.

A new iron kettle may be cleaned by boiling in it a good-sized handful of hay.

Anchovy fillets rolled in nutmeg and chopped mint leaves is a good appetizer.

Ginger poultices, instead of mustard, will relieve neuralgia and will not blister.

A fine substitute for sour cream can be made by beating together until perfectly smooth two parts of cottage cheese to one part of buttermilk.

Think of olives as a staple food rather than something to put in a martini. Combine them (try both black and green) with veal, fish, or egg dishes; drop a handful into a stew.

Remember the advice of Brillat-Savarin: "The discovery of a new dish does more for the happiness of man than the discovery of a star."

Fry tomatoes in pure olive oil and minced garlic and serve with French bread.

Vanilla beans, used to flavor milk or custard, can be washed, dried, and stored for re-use.

Try Danish squash filled with peas, tiny onions, mushrooms, and meat gravy—baked.

Seventeenth-century princes sent each other potatoes as a curiosity.

Tag ends of jam can be brought back to life with a little hot water and brandy.

So can dried fruits that have been allowed to sit on the shelf too long.

Sweep the floor every day and keep a pot of geraniums at the window.

For Sunday breakfast, top oatmeal with brown sugar and a splash of rum. Ignite.

Always buy *fresh* rolls.

And always cook with *butter*!

THE NICKEL DINNER AND HOW IT'S CHANGED

Over the years the nickel dinner has changed—in price, for one thing. Today a nickel is good for a parking meter, a stick of bubble gum, or a piggy bank. It will not provide much nourishment.

It—the nickel (5¢) dinner—is a memory cast off along the route as were the plastic-handled flatware and the soft Mexican pottery. Almost forgotten.

But, as do the French knife and a few cherished kitchen tools, the concept remains: the Poor Poet (and others) can eat better for less, be it a simple supper, a bountiful feast, or a worthwhile snack.

So, too, the original rules remain:

> Always have fresh bread.
> Always use butter.
> Always serve wine.
> Have a candle for the table.

Changes have called for new rules.

Rule One. Meat is not the *only* protein. I had always eaten lots of red meat. ("Finish your meat, Ann, so you will grow strong and healthy.") I did grow strong and healthy and—eventually—a bit fat. Then meat prices soared, made headline news. I could not blame the local butcher; he was, after all, my friend. I blamed the politicians and, in lieu of writing scathing letters, all but stopped eating meat.

Generations of Poor Poets and those not so poor were my mentors. I delved into Rousseau and Shaw and Gandhi and Singer. I studied the Hindus and Buddhists and unearthed obscure societies around the world. I pondered the dishes of other countries—in which a little meat goes a long way or is used sparingly, much as an herb, to add flavor.

And as my library grew, my kitchen changed. There were jars of seeds and nuts and beans and rice. And pasta of every sort. The refrigerator meat drawer was relabeled "Cheese." It took time and poking around in Oriental and Mexican and Middle Eastern markets, as well as in the "natural foods" stores—a new one around almost any corner.

I had fun. Shopping and cooking were new adventures. I spent less money and grew less fat. And—contrary to the dire warnings of self-appointed advisers—I continued strong and healthy.

Rule Two. Throw out the salt. Not all of it, but begin cutting down. And never, never put salt on the table, even though the pepper mill does look lonely without its mate.

Rule Three. Hide the sugar. Unearth it only to build a diabolical dessert or make jam or apple butter.

Rule Four. Cut down on convenience and processed foods.

These are the new rules. Unlike the original ones of bread, butter, wine, and a candle for the table, they are flexible. They are to aid the Poor Poet (and others) to concentrate on clean and simple tastes much as, in studio or loft, the goal is the flawless brush stroke, the succinct word, the single clear note.

SOUPS

*Beautiful Soup! Who cares for fish,
Game, or any other dish!*
—Lewis Carroll

More Hot Soups for Cold Days

POOR POET'S PEASANT SOUP   6–8

4 medium onions
4 large potatoes
10 chicken bouillon cubes
5 cups water
3 whole cloves
¼ teaspoon pepper
½ teaspoon each thyme and marjoram leaves
½ pound green beans
½ pound bacon
¼ cup pitted green olives
6 thick slices French bread
¼ pound mozzarella cheese, grated

Peel and quarter the onions and slice the potatoes thickly. Place them in a pot with the bouillon cubes, water, cloves, pepper, and herbs. Cover and simmer 45 minutes, adding the cut-up green beans after half an hour. In the meantime dice the bacon, fry it almost crisp, and drain well. Halve the olives and add them, with the bacon, to the pot.

Sprinkle the cheese on the bread and toast it, in a 350° oven, until the cheese melts.

Ladle the soup into generous bowls. (Do try to locate and discard the three cloves.) Top each serving with toast.

SANTA FE POTATO-TOMATO SOUP   6–8

8 *potatoes*	1 *small red chili pepper*
6 *tomatoes*	1 *green pepper*
2 *onions*	*several sprigs parsley*
1 *quart water*	½ *teaspoon salt*

Dice the potatoes and tomatoes and slice the onions. Simmer in water for an hour, or until almost tender. Now crush the chili pepper, slice the green pepper, and chop the parsley. Add them, along with the salt, and cook for about 5 additional minutes. Tortilla chips go perfectly with this soup.

GRANDMOTHER'S YELLOW PEA SOUP   6

Years ago my neighbor (we are always there if one or the other needs an onion or an egg) gave me her recipe for pea soup. In due course I forgot that it included ham. So she wrote out the recipe again, along with one of her grandmother's favorite sayings: "One wit, like a knuckle of ham in soup, gives a zest and flavour to the dish, but more than one serves only to spoil the pottage." The lines, she said, were from Smollett and perhaps would jog my memory.

8 *cups water*	2 *stalks celery, sliced*
2 *cups dried* whole *yellow peas*	1 *ham bone or* 2 *tablespoons ham or bacon fat*
4 *large cloves garlic*	½ *teaspoon salt*
2 *carrots, sliced*	*pepper*

Combine all ingredients, cover, and simmer 2 hours, stirring occasionally. Remove the bone and press the mixture through a sieve. If there is meat on the bone, cut it in small pieces and return it to the soup.

MARY'S CHEESE AND VEGETABLE CHOWDER ৫ 4–6

When Mary isn't swamped with slips from the adding machine and messages from the computer, her mind turns to Poor Poet things like discovering new places or working out new recipes. Because she's fond of cheese, she pops it into lots of dishes, including soup.

4 *large zucchini*
1 *medium onion*
2 *tablespoons minced parsley*
1 *teaspoon basil*
¼ *cup butter*
¼ *cup flour*
4 *chicken bouillon cubes*
3 *cups water*
1 *teaspoon lemon juice*
1 *10-ounce package frozen corn or baby limas*
1¾ *cups rich milk*
1 *1-pound, 4-ounce can tomatoes*
1 *cup shredded fontina or Cheddar cheese*
¼ *cup grated Romano cheese*
salt and pepper

Slice the zucchini and chop the onion. Cook and stir, along with the parsley and basil, in butter for 5 minutes. Stir in the flour and cook for a few minutes. Add bouillon cubes, water, and lemon juice. When the stock is boiling, add the corn and simmer for 5 or 6 additional minutes. Add the remaining ingredients in order, cooking and stirring until the cheeses are melted. Season with salt and pepper.

VIPAVSKA CORBA ৫ 8–10

Here is a sturdy soup from the forests of Slovenia. The recipe is easily halved; it is also easily doubled, provided one has a large enough pot. The basic cooking can be done ahead and the soup put together in a few minutes. And, if bacon is too dear, the quantity can be reduced.

1 *pound small white beans*　　1 *large onion*
1 *two-pound jar sauerkraut*　　3 *cloves garlic*
1 *pound slab bacon*　　2 *or* 3 *bay leaves*
1 *pound potatoes*　　*salt and pepper*
1 *tablespoon fat*　　*sour cream or yogurt*
1 *tablespoon flour*

Soak the beans overnight. Remove the rind from the bacon but leave it in one piece. Cut the potatoes into small chunks. Cook the beans, bacon, and potatoes separately. Keep the stock!

Chop onion and garlic and sauté them in one tablespoon of the fat that has risen to the top of the bacon stock. Sprinkle in flour and stir. Then add the beans, potatoes, sauerkraut, bacon that has been cut in dice, bay leaves, salt, and pepper. Add more water if necessary. Cover and cook until heated through. Top each serving with sour cream or yogurt.

Accompany the Corba with dark bread or rye crackers and butter, and a mixed vegetable salad. Fruit and coffee follow.

OUT-OF-THE-CUPBOARD SOUP　　ช 4–6

1 10½-*ounce can condensed*　　1 *soup can water*
　cream of chicken soup　　½ *cup chopped peanuts*
1 10½-*ounce can condensed*　　¼ *cup chopped pimiento*
　cream of mushroom soup　　1 *tablespoon chopped*
1 *soup can milk*　　　*parsley*

Blend the soups, milk, and water in a saucepan and add the remaining ingredients. Heat slowly, stirring occasionally.

More Cold Soups for Hot Days

CUCUMBER-WALNUT SOUP ↻ 6

1 quart plain yogurt or
   buttermilk
½ cup chicken stock
2 cucumbers, diced
¼ teaspoon garlic powder
   salt and pepper
1 cup chopped walnuts

If using yogurt, beat it until it is smooth before stirring in the stock, cucumbers, garlic, salt, and pepper. Buttermilk can simply be poured right into the bowl. Chill for several hours. Top each serving with chopped walnuts.

EMBARCADERO FISH SOUP ↻ 6

½ pound cooked fish or
   shellfish
¼ cup lime juice
¼ cup chopped onion
1½ cups tomato juice
2 cups clam juice or
   chicken broth
1 teaspoon minced
   parsley
½ cup chopped green
   pepper
   Tabasco

Combine all ingredients and chill well. This soup should have *bite* to it, so don't hold back on the Tabasco. Chinese parsley (fresh coriander) and chopped green chilies, if available, can replace the regular parsley and Tabasco.

A Jar of Bouillon Cubes

Among those things that the Poor Poet might consider "staples" is a jar of bouillon cubes—chicken is my favorite, but there are usually beef and vegetable, too. This little store, plus pre-planning or searching in the refrigerator or garden, is the basis for sudden soups almost without end. To wit:

SPRINGTIME BOUILLON

Drop a few fresh or frozen peas, a sliced green onion, and several asparagus tips into simmering chicken bouillon. Cook only until the vegetables are tender-crisp.

GREEN BROTH

Whisk together a small egg, a heaping tablespoon of bread crumbs, and some chopped parsley. Stir this into simmering chicken bouillon. Squeeze in a bit of lemon juice before serving.

LEMON SOUP

Add cooked rice to simmering chicken stock along with a pinch each of basil, mint, and thyme. Beat an egg yolk with the juice of one lemon and a little stock. Stir this into the bouillon and cook until thickened.

MUSHROOM-NOODLE SOUP

Sauté a handful of sliced mushrooms, a sliced green onion, and a crushed clove of garlic in butter. Add water, chicken bouillon cubes, and a few broken egg noodles. Cover and simmer until the noodles are tender. Season with cracked pepper.

BOUILLON WITH LIME AND TORTILLA CHIPS

Squeeze lots of lime juice into steaming chicken bouillon. Serve with a basket of tortilla chips, which are broken up and added in the process of eating.

BOUILLON WITH SHELLS

Simmer small shell pasta in chicken bouillon until they are just tender. Top each serving with sour cream and a sprinkling of dill weed.

SALADS

There was a time when I really considered myself a purist. It was a time of being more poor than poet and when all salads had to be green and tossed at the table *at the very last minute*—with a flourish. Otherwise, hysteria ensued. I even owned a salad basket that I would swing wildly around my head. It was all very preachy and superior.

The truth dawned. (Perhaps the salad basket klonked me on the head.) I was expending a lot of energy and I was missing a lot.

The green salad, tossed at the table *at the very last minute*, has not been abandoned. In fact, it frequently appears. But Poor Poets (especially those who lack stoves or who live in hot climates) might well consider salads that—along with a cup of bouillon, a glass of wine, and bread and butter—constitute a whole meal.

BLACK FOREST SPINACH AND ALMOND SALAD

↺ 4

1½ *bunches spinach*
4 *slices bacon*
2 *tablespoons kirsch**
2 *tablespoons red currant jelly*

1 *tablespoon vinegar*
⅔ *cup sliced toasted almonds*

* 2 tablespoons orange juice and 1 teaspoon vinegar may substitute for the kirsch.

Wash, tear, and dry spinach. Fry bacon until crisp, then drain on a paper towel and crumble. *Save the bacon fat.* For the dressing, drain off all but 3 tablespoons bacon fat from the skillet. Add kirsch, jelly, and vinegar, and quickly bring to a boil. Sprinkle the bacon and almonds over the spinach, drizzle with dressing, and toss gently.

CALLIGRAPHER'S CABBAGE ↺ 4
AND HAM

A salad of Japanese origin to be served warm, perhaps with a bowl of steamed rice, or cold with flour tortillas.

1¾ *pounds cabbage or* *Brussels sprouts*	4 *tablespoons Japanese* *rice wine or white*
2 *or* 3 *slices ham*	*wine vinegar*
3 *tablespoons sesame* *seeds*	½ *teaspoon salt*
	1 *tablespoon sugar*
	1 *teaspoon soy sauce*

Shred the cabbage as fine as possible, cook quickly so that it is still crisp, and drain well. Shred the ham. Parch the sesame seeds by shaking them in a covered pan over medium heat. Crush them and add the vinegar, salt, sugar, and soy. Toss well with the cabbage and ham.

A SENSUOUS SALAD

For this salad (which should not be eaten while wearing one's best shirt—the bean sprouts have a way of flipping oil at random) measurements are by handful and eye.

very crisp bean sprouts	*olive oil*
celery	*lemon juice*
sunflower seeds	*salt and pepper*
crumbled bacon or bacon *bits*	

For each handful of sprouts use a large stalk of celery, diced, and about 2 tablespoons each of sunflower seeds and bacon. Sprinkle with salt and pepper, and toss with olive oil and lemon juice.

PICNIC IN THE PARK TOMATOES ♋ 8

8 *large tomatoes*
¼ *cup olive oil*
1 *cup chopped onion*
2 *cloves garlic, minced*
1¼ *cups diced eggplant*
2 *or 3 zucchini, cubed*
2 *green peppers, sliced*
1 *teaspoon oregano*
salt and pepper

Hollow the tomatoes and set them aside. Simmer the tomato pulp with the other ingredients until the vegetables are barely tender. Cool and stuff into the tomato cases. Chill for several hours.

If the tomatoes are, indeed, going to the park, secure each one well in plastic wrap. Whether they are eaten indoors or out, they are best accompanied with cheese or sausage, French bread and butter, and red wine.

EXPATRIATE'S CHEESE SALAD ♋ 4

A writer who lives on a nearby hillside moved to a Swiss village not long ago. But because she so liked to eat, her days were spent investigating the markets. So she returned with a still-unfinished manuscript *but* several fine recipes.

¾ *pound Swiss cheese*
2 *cups shredded red or*
  green cabbage
1 *carrot*
1 *stalk celery*
1 *bunch radishes*
1 *green pepper*
1 *tomato*
1 *or 2 hard-cooked eggs*
salad oil
tarragon vinegar
1 *teaspoon prepared*
  mustard
salt and pepper

Slice the cheese, vegetables, and eggs. Toss with oil and vinegar, mustard, salt, and pepper. Serve on a bed of lettuce. Crusty bread with butter is a must, and—for some reason—beer or sparkling cider instead of wine.

LITTLE RIVER SALAD ↻ 6

Little River is just south of Mendocino. By now Poor Poets outnumber lumberjacks, and on sunny days there are suppers on the terrace or—if the fog blows in—in front of the fireplace.

2 *one-pound cans garbanzos*
2 *7-ounce cans tuna*
1 *can anchovy fillets*
4 *tomatoes*
1 *onion*
4 *hard-cooked eggs*
1 *clove garlic*
1 *pound green beans, cooked tender-crisp*
$\frac{1}{2}$ *cup chopped parsley*
1 *tablespoon basil*
olive oil
vinegar
salt and pepper

Drain the garbanzos, tuna, and anchovy fillets. Slice the tomatoes, onion, and eggs, and mince the garlic. Toss all the ingredients in a large bowl with oil and vinegar.

JOHN'S SALAD

During lunch breaks at a recent conference some of us who prefer our own cooking to the nearby fast food offerings found ourselves sharing an impromptu pot luck. Each day John brought a rather dented roasting pan filled with salad, and his friend brought a jar of dressing.

The salad was never quite the same, but it did contain most or all of the following:

lettuce
sliced celery
green pepper strips
sliced raw mushrooms
diced apple

grated carrots
soy-toasted sunflower seeds
and peanuts (page 204)
currants

AN ANTIPASTO ↺ 6

1 cup green beans
2 cups peas
4 new potatoes
1 can artichoke hearts
　olive oil
　lemon juice
1 teaspoon dried tarragon

salt and pepper
½ cup mayonnaise
1 teaspoon prepared
　mustard
2 cucumbers
2 hard-cooked eggs
1 tablespoon capers

Cook the beans, peas, and potatoes separately. Drain. Slice the potatoes and drain and halve the artichokes. Marinate the vegetables in olive oil and lemon juice seasoned with tarragon, salt, and pepper. Just before serving, toss the marinated vegetables with the mayonnaise and mustard. Slice the cucumbers around the edge of the dish and top it with sliced eggs and capers.

SUM AND SUBSTANCE

Eggs and Cheese

*The farmer's daughter hath soft brown hair
(Butter and eggs and a pound of cheese)
And I met with a ballad, I can't say where
That wholly consisted of lines like these.*
—CHARLES S. CALVERLY, *Ballad*

AN OMELET WITH CRUNCH ✌ 1

2 eggs
1 teaspoon water
salt
2 dashes Tabasco
2 tablespoons butter
3 slices tomato
3 slices avocado
$\frac{1}{4}$ cup alfalfa sprouts
$\frac{1}{4}$ cup yogurt
1 tablespoon chopped walnuts

Whisk together the eggs, water, salt, and Tabasco. Heat the butter in an omelet pan, and as the bubbles subside, pour in the egg mixture. Shake and tilt the pan until the eggs are set but the top is still creamy. Arrange the remaining ingredients on half the omelet and roll it out onto a warm plate.

FONDUE BRILLAT-SAVARIN

A politican by vocation, Brillat-Savarin is remembered less for the writings in his field than for his still-timely *La Physiologie du Goût*. A true Poor Poet spirit.

Somewhere, long ago, I stumbled upon his formula (it can hardly be called a recipe) for fondue. It is superb.

Weigh the eggs. Weigh Gruyère to one-third the weight of the eggs, and butter to one-sixth their weight. Beat the eggs; add the cheese and butter finely diced. Put into a hot, lightly buttered pan, turning the mixture with a small spatula until it is thick but still soft. Serve immediately, seasoned only with freshly ground pepper.

FLEMISH EGGS   ɔ 4

And changing like a poet's rhymes,
Rang the beautiful wild chimes
From the Belfry in the market
Of the ancient town of Bruges.

Recite a bit of Longfellow and prepare this dish, a very old recipe from the city of which he writes.

2 *tablespoons butter*	1 *teaspoon dry mustard*
8 *large hard-cooked eggs*	1½ *cups cream or rich milk*
4 *ounces baby shrimp*	*salt and pepper*
1 *teaspoon chervil*	½ *cup grated cheese (i.e.,*
1 *tablespoon parsley*	*Swiss or Gruyère)*

Melt the butter in a saucepan. Shell and shred eggs into the butter. Add all ingredients except the cheese and mix gently with a fork. Divide the mixture among four buttered au gratin dishes or ramekins. Sprinkle cheese on top, and a bit more butter if desired. Place in a 375° oven for 10 minutes or until hot and bubbly and the top begins to brown. Serve with French bread, a tossed salad, and white wine.

BLINTZWICHES ↄ 6

1 cup cottage cheese
4 eggs
1 teaspoon sugar
12 slices bread
⅓ cup milk

2 tablespoons butter
applesauce, cranberry sauce, jam, or sour cream

    Combine cottage cheese with one egg and sugar. Stir well. Use this to fill six sandwiches. Beat the remaining eggs with the milk. Heat the butter in a skillet. Quickly dip each Blintzwich in the egg-milk mixture. Sauté until lightly browned on both sides. Serve with apple or cranberry sauce, jam or sour cream.

A ONE-POT FROM ATHENS ↄ 6

2 medium zucchini
1 small eggplant (1½ pounds)
1 large onion
⅓ cup olive oil
1 16-ounce can tomatoes

2 tablespoons chopped mint
2 teaspoons dill weed
salt and pepper
¾ cup yogurt
¾ pound feta cheese

    Slice the zucchini, dice the eggplant, and chop the onion. Sauté for 5 minutes in olive oil. Add tomatoes, mint, dill, salt, and pepper. Cover and cook 10 minutes or until the vegetables are just tender. Stir in the yogurt. Crumble cheese on top just before serving.

    This one-pot can be served on macaroni or with French bread and butter. It is also fun, albeit a bit drippy, to spoon into heated pocket bread.

SUPPER AT THE SPA NUT LOAF ↄ 8

    We once stumbled upon a spa whose clientele was more interested in getting away to read, to write, to compose, or to listen than to follow a stringent health routine. Because everyone demanded the recipe, its

EGGS AND CHEESE

inventor posted it on the bulletin board with a little addendum: "You can add any grated vegetables, cooked lentils, raw oats, etc.—"

2 *small onions*	2 *cups grated cheese*
2 *tablespoons butter*	1½ *cups chopped walnuts*
3 *eggs*	*juice of one lemon*
milk or water	2 *tablespoons wheat germ*
1½ *cups whole wheat bread crumbs*	

Chop the onions and sauté them in butter until golden. Beat the eggs with a little milk or water and combine all ingredients except the wheat germ. Press gently into a well-buttered loaf pan and top with wheat germ. Bake at 350° for 30 minutes or until the loaf is set and the top has browned.

Hot tomato sauce or white sauce to which additional butter has been added can be served over each slice.

Peas, Beans, Rice, and Grains

A letter dated "Wyoming Territory, 1883," contains this lament: "I've had the most terrible journey 4 days by wagon and nothing but *beans* . . ." Perhaps the cook lacked imagination; more likely, he had nothing to put with the beans.

For Poor Poets, peas, beans, rice, and grains are staples. So are the herbs, spices, and seasonings that turn these staples into something special.

CAJUN STEW

2 cups dry lentils
4 slices bacon
2 large onions
4 cloves garlic
1 green pepper
3 stalks celery
6 vegetable bouillon cubes
1 28-ounce can sliced tomatoes
1 14-ounce can okra
3 bay leaves
¼ teaspoon thyme
salt, cayenne, and Tabasco to taste

Soak the lentils overnight and drain. Dice the bacon, chop the onions, garlic, green pepper, and celery, and sauté until golden. Add the other ingredients with enough hot water to cover. Simmer for 30 minutes, checking to see that the pot has not become too dry.

Serve Cajun Stew over rice, dashing on additional Tabasco to taste. Or, if more than six or eight hungry poets turn up, add water and bouillon cubes to the pot and have Cajun *Soup*, accompanied by lots of crusty French bread for dunking.

LEEWARD ISLANDS GARBANZO STEW ≈ 6

3 cups dry garbanzos
½ pound salt pork
½ pound ham
1 large onion
2 cloves garlic
¼ pound sausage meat
6 peppercorns
1 whole clove
12 small potatoes
1 medium head cabbage
salt, pepper, and Tabasco

Soak garbanzos overnight in water. Dice the salt pork and ham, chop the onion and garlic, and sauté these, with the sausage, until golden. Add the garbanzos with enough of their soaking water to cover. Tie the peppercorns and clove in cheesecloth and drop into the pot. Cover and simmer for about an hour and a half. Place the potatoes over the stew. Shred the cabbage on top.

Cover and continue cooking for at least another half hour. Season to taste with salt and pepper. Let each person determine how much Tabasco is added to his plate.

TACU TACU ≈ 6

3 *cups mashed kidney beans*	2 *fresh or canned green chilies*
2 *cups cooked rice*	4 *tablespoons oil*
1 *onion*	*salt and pepper*
1 *small tomato*	6 *fried eggs (for hungry poets)*

Mix the beans and rice. Chop the vegetables and sauté them for a few minutes in the oil. Add the bean-rice mixture, the salt and pepper, and stir well. Press the Tacu Tacu with a spatula so that it will hold its shape. When it is brown on one side slide it onto a plate and back into the pan to brown the other side. Cut in wedges and serve with or without fried eggs.

RUSSIAN KASHA ≈ 6

1 *egg*	1 *cup sliced mushrooms*
1 *cup buckwheat groats*	$\frac{1}{2}$ *cup sliced celery*
1 *teaspoon salt*	1 *onion, sliced*
$1\frac{1}{2}$ *teaspoons thyme*	1 *cup sour cream or yogurt*
$\frac{1}{2}$ *teaspoon marjoram*	*hard-cooked eggs (optional)*
2 *cups boiling water or stock*	
$\frac{1}{4}$ *cup butter*	

Beat the egg and mix in the groats. Pour the mixture into a large skillet and heat until dry, stirring constantly. Add the salt (if using stock instead of water, cut down on the amount), thyme, marjoram, and boiling water. Stir, cover, and simmer 20 minutes.

Sauté the vegetables in butter for 5 minutes, then add

them to the groats mixture, along with more water if it seems dry. Simmer 10 minutes longer.

Serve with sour cream or yogurt. Hard-cooked eggs, sliced over each serving, turn this into a whole meal.

PILAF WITH ALMONDS ~ 4–6

2 cups chicken stock
1 cup cracked wheat
¼ teaspoon salt
½ teaspoon basil
¼ teaspoon mint leaves
½ teaspoon grated lemon rind
½ cup almonds
3 tablespoons butter
½ cup sliced green onions
⅓ cup raisins
2 tablespoons chopped parsley
1 tablespoon lemon juice
1 cup diced cooked lamb or poultry or 1½ cups fried eggplant cubes or diced tomatoes

Put chicken stock in a pan and add cracked wheat, salt, basil, mint, and lemon rind. Heat to boiling. Cover, turn heat to low, and cook 15 minutes. Meanwhile chop the almonds and brown lightly in butter, stirring constantly. When the wheat is cooked, add nuts, onions, raisins, parsley, and lemon juice. Toss lightly to mix. Add the meat or vegetables and heat only a minute or so longer.

RICE PIE ~ 6

Instead of a pastry shell that too often ends up with a soggy bottom, try a rice shell.

SHELL

2 cups cooked rice
2 tablespoons melted butter
1 beaten egg
1 tablespoon chopped onion
¼ teaspoon marjoram

Combine the ingredients and press into bottom and sides of a buttered 10-inch pie plate.

FILLING

1 cup drained tuna,　　　1 cup milk
　flaked fish, or leftover　3 eggs, beaten
　poultry or ham　　　　　$\frac{1}{4}$ teaspoon marjoram
1 cup shredded Swiss　　　1 tablespoon chopped onion
　cheese　　　　　　　　　salt and pepper

Pour the filling into the shell. Bake at 350° for 50 minutes or until a knife inserted near the center comes out clean.

MAMALIGA　　　　　　　　　　　　　　　　ᖱ 4–6

Just as Poor Poets (and others) flying east tuck loaves of San Francisco sourdough bread under their arms, Poor Poets leaving Philadelphia tote carefully wrapped packages of scrapple. And although that city might have a corner on the name, there are other scrapples to consider. Here is one from Romania.

1½ cups cornmeal　　　　　chopped hard-cooked
　pinch of salt　　　　　　　eggs, grated cheese
　any one or more: cubed　　butter
　ham, diced bacon,　　　　sour cream or yogurt
　sliced mushrooms,

Cook cornmeal according to package directions. When it is done, fold in whatever and howmuchever you want of ham, etc. Pour into a greased 1-quart mold and chill. Slice the Mamaliga, brown in butter, and serve with sour cream or yogurt.

Pasta

An intriguing idea: a land where cooks stand on mounds of Parmesan cheese and ladle macaroni and ravioli into pots of capon broth. It was not dreamed up today, but at the turn of the fourteenth century by Giovanni Boccaccio. It merits thought.

PASTA VERDE ↻ 6

1 *pound spaghetti or green noodles*
1 *pound spinach*
1 *clove garlic*
¼ *cup olive oil*
¼ *cup chopped parsley*
1 *tablespoon sunflower seeds*
¼ *cup chopped toasted almonds*
¼ *teaspoon basil*
1½ *cups yogurt*
grated Parmesan

Boil pasta to al dente stage. Chop the spinach and mince the garlic. Drain the pasta in a colander. Put the oil and all other ingredients except yogurt and Parmesan into the pot and sauté until the vegetables are barely limp. Blend in the yogurt. Return the pasta to the pot and toss gently but thoroughly. Serve accompanied by a bowl of grated Parmesan.

Unless you are looking for a truly all-green dinner, plan a salad that includes beets and perhaps a handful of pitted black olives.

NANCY'S OWN ORIGINAL SPAGHETTI MARCO POLO ↻ 6

The lengthy title for this excellent spaghetti alludes to the fact that the recipe has been stolen at least once. "Word for word—even the title," I told Nancy. She laughed and said she'd no idea how she came to concoct it in the first place and that she now put it in my hands.

1 *pound spaghetti*
1 *cup chopped nuts (walnuts, peanuts, sunflower seeds)*
⅔ *cup chopped black olives*
½ *cup chopped red pimiento or red bell pepper*
½ *cup chopped parsley*
1 *teaspoon (or more) chopped fresh basil*
salt and pepper
4–5 *tablespoons olive oil*
3–4 *garlic cloves, crushed*
grated Parmesan

Boil pasta to al dente stage. While it boils, combine nuts, olives, pimiento, parsley, basil, and salt and pepper to taste. Drain pasta into a large colander. Put oil and garlic into the pot and cook over moderate heat for 1 minute. Return pasta to pot and blend thoroughly with oil-garlic mixture. Top with herb-nut mixture and toss gently. Serve at once. Pass a bowl of Parmesan to be sprinkled on top.

Fish

"When I ask him what he is doing, he replies
that he is looking at the Virgin of the Carmen,
who appears, with her open embroidered
mantle, under the rainbow, on the scale;
the Virgin of the Carmen, patron saint of seamen . . ."
—Juan Ramón Jiménez, *Platero and I*

FISH BAKED WITH LEMONS AND ONIONS ↻ 4

2 pounds white fish fillets
¼ cup mayonnaise
3 lemons
2 large onions

paprika
salt and pepper
½ cup dry white wine or vermouth

Brush the bottom of a baking pan with half the mayonnaise. Slice lemons paper-thin and arrange in the bottom of the pan. Lay the fish fillets over the lemons. Brush them with the remaining mayonnaise. Slice the onions and strew them over the fish. Season with a little paprika, salt, and pepper. Sprinkle white wine over all. Bake at 350° for 30 minutes or until the fish flakes when tested with a fork.

FISH BAKED WITH POTATOES ℞ 6

2 pounds white fish fillets
4 large potatoes
1 large Spanish onion
½ stick butter
¼ cup flour
2½ teaspoons paprika
1 tablespoon dill weed
⅛ teaspoon thyme
salt and pepper
1 cup milk
¼ cup minced parsley

Peel and thinly slice the potatoes and lay them in the bottom of a buttered baking pan. Top with thin-sliced onion and thin slices of butter. Arrange the fish over the vegetables. Sprinkle the flour and seasonings over all. Bake the dish for 10 minutes at 450°, then lower the temperature to 350° and pour half the milk over the fish. Continue baking for about 30 minutes or until the potatoes are tender and the fish flakes when tested with a fork. Baste from time to time and add additional milk if the dish tends to dryness. Sprinkle parsley over the dish just before serving.

SAVE THE FAMILY ℞ 6

Not only can this dish save the family; it can also save leftovers from wasting away. Try other fish or shellfish and other vegetables.

4 large potatoes, baked or boiled
½ cup buttermilk
2 tablespoons butter
salt and pepper
1 teaspoon dill weed
1 pound cooked shrimp
4 hard-cooked eggs
2 large tomatoes
2 cups cooked peas
2 cups cooked beets
½ cup toasted bread crumbs
a simple oil and vinegar dressing

Peel the potatoes and break them up on a buttered baking dish. Pour buttermilk over the potatoes, dot with butter, and sprinkle with salt, pepper, and dill. Arrange shrimp, quartered eggs, tomato wedges, peas, and beets on top. Sprinkle with bread crumbs. Slip under the broiler to heat thoroughly. Serve with the oil and vinegar dressing on the side.

Miscellanea

Watch for little miracles. They arrive as from nowhere—just pop into being. Or they arrive in the mail, tucked among advertisements and bills, as did Brenda's recipe for Mushrooms on Toast.

MUSHROOMS ON TOAST ‿ 4

1 *pound mushrooms*
¼ *stick butter*
4 *tablespoons chopped celery*
3 *tablespoons chopped green onion*
2 *tablespoons chopped parsley*
1 *clove garlic, mashed*
1½ *teaspoons MSG*
salt and pepper
½ *teaspoon ginger*

Remove stems from mushrooms and chop. Halve or quarter the caps, depending on size. Melt butter in a frying pan that can be tightly covered and add the vegetables and MSG. Steam-fry for 5 to 10 minutes. Season with salt, pepper, and ginger just before serving on buttered toast.

Mushrooms on Toast may be served, with equal success, on rice or noodles.

POOR POET'S CURRY

Here is a curry sauce for simmering all sorts of things. Cooked and drained soybeans, garbanzos, or black-eyed peas are one. Raw vegetables such as eggplant cubes, cauliflower flowerets, peas and cubed potatoes, sliced zucchini and carrots, or green beans and mushrooms are another. Shrimp, firm white fish, or strips of chicken breast are yet one more.

2 tablespoons butter	1 tablespoon curry powder
½ cup chopped onions	1½ cups chicken or
1 tablespoon grated ginger root	vegetable bouillon

Heat the butter in a saucepan (or frying pan with lid), add the onions and ginger root, and stir and fry until the onions are golden. Now stir in the curry powder and let cook for a minute. Add the bouillon and, when the sauce begins to simmer, toss in about 2 cups beans, vegetables, shrimp, or whatever. Cover the pan, lower the heat, and cook only until the contents are tender.

The amount of curry powder to use depends not only on individual taste but on the strength of the powder itself. Yogurt (perhaps a half cupful) can replace a bit of the bouillon and is particularly good for vegetable curry.

HERBES DE PROVENCE

One of my favorite herb combinations, this brings to mind warm vineyards and pastures waist-deep in flowers. In France the herbs are often pressed thickly around little sausages before they are hung to dry. At home I use it quite frequently on broiled chicken.

To prepare, simply crush equal parts of fennel seed, thyme, basil, savory, and lavender in a mortar. Crush the fennel seeds first so as not to pulverize the leaves of the other herbs.

GOMA-SHIO

Only a few minutes are required to prepare a jar of crunchy sesame seeds and salt, called Goma-Shio in

Japan. It is excellent sprinkled over salads, cooked vegetables, or rice.

Make small batches at a time and store in the refrigerator to insure freshness.

½ *cup sesame seeds*
1 *tablespoon salt*

Measure the seeds and salt into a skillet with a lid. Cook over low heat, shaking the pan all the while, until the seeds are golden brown. (The lid is to keep the tiny seeds from popping all over the stove.)

Crush with a mortar and pestle or with the back of a wooden spoon until the mixture is just crumbly.

CHINESE FIVE SPICES

Oriental recipes often call for "Five Spices," a product not always readily available. The mixture is excellent for seasoning pot roast, broiled chicken, or roast pork. It is interesting on salad, if used with caution.

Make a little and, if you become addicted, increase the measurements the next time around.

1 *part each ground ginger and dry mustard*
½ *part each salt and finely ground pepper*
¼ *part powdered anise*

APPLESAUCE

I have yet to see anyone refuse to eat a raw apple because there is no sugar, cinnamon, or nutmeg to be sprinkled on. Why, then, add all these things to applesauce?

Admittedly, my applesauce-making method was born of necessity: the tree had produced a huge crop, and I was pressed to get the sauce made and into the freezer with as little fuss as possible.

Wash, quarter, and core apples. Chop them (including the peel) well or grate them. A food processor or an electric mixer with a grating attachment—if one is so affluent to own either—saves considerable effort. Dump the apples into a pan, add only enough water to prevent burning, cover, and bring quickly to a boil. Cook until the apples are just tender. Cool and store in the refrigerator, or freeze.

Three Snacks for the Poor Poet's Work Space

My friend who creates all sorts of things at Windy Gap once asked why I didn't do a chapter or article on eating while working, and I replied that, although both activities are enjoyable, I prefer to keep them separate.

Nevertheless, there is no reason why the Poor Poet cannot have a basket of fruit or a jar of snacks close at hand. Here are three snacks that can help prevent one from wearing a path between work space and kitchen.

GINGER BALLS

1 *cup each sunflower seeds, raisins, pitted dates, and prunes*
$\frac{1}{2}$ *cup crystallized ginger*
1 *cup sesame seeds*

Chop sunflower seeds and set aside. Now chop or grind the fruits and ginger and combine with the sunflower seeds. Form into walnut-sized balls and roll in sesame seeds. Wrap individually in plastic wrap or pile into a cookie tin with plastic wrap between each layer.

HONEYED GRAPEFRUIT RIND

    rind from 4 or 5   1½ *cups honey*
      grapefruits (or oranges)   1 *cup grated unsweetened*
    4 *cups water*   *coconut*
    1 *tablespoon salt*

    Cut the rind into strips and soak it overnight in salt water. Drain, rinse, and soak in fresh water for 20 minutes. Drain again, cover with fresh water, and simmer for 20 minutes. Allow the peel to drain for an hour or so. Then toss it into a saucepan, add the honey, and simmer very slowly for 45 minutes or until the rind is clear. Spread the slices on plastic wrap or a cake rack and allow to dry for 3 or 4 days. Roll the rind in coconut and store in a tight container, separating the layers with plastic wrap.

SOY-TOASTED SEEDS AND NUTS

    Sunflower seeds, pumpkin seeds, and all sorts of nuts (but especially almonds) become something very special when soaked in soy sauce and then toasted.
    If doing more than one kind of seed or nut at a time, keep them separated. Pour whatever is to be toasted into a bowl and sprinkle liberally with soy sauce. Soak for several hours or overnight, stirring occasionally. Drain in a strainer; pour any excess soy sauce into a bottle for future use.
    Spread the seeds or nuts on a baking sheet and toast in a 225° oven until they are crisp. Stir occasionally. Each variety has its own time limit for doneness—from 30 minutes to over 1 hour. Cool and store in jars, preferably in the refrigerator.

DESSERTS

By now everyone has heard the word: "Avoid refined sugar like the plague." Some go so far as to include honey and molasses in the "plague" warning. Difficult advice, indeed, for those with a lifetime history of dessert eating.

When I was eight years old my father and I concocted a monumental dessert. We layered vanilla ice cream, chocolate sauce, and salted peanuts in a tall glass and beamed at each other as we attacked it with Mother's best iced-tea spoons. Such was life—then.

Today dessert is often fresh or dried fruits with, perhaps, a few nuts. But sometimes this Spartan and healthy regime gives way. So, to fit whatever the whim, some of the desserts offered here are virtuous, some are not so virtuous, and two are utterly wicked.

Some Virtuous Desserts

FRUIT BOWL KIPLING   4

2 *bananas*
2 *oranges*
½ *cup slivered dates*
2 *cups pineapple chunks*
curry powder
½ *cup chopped salted peanuts*

Slice the bananas into a bowl. Peel the oranges, cut them into bite-size pieces of half moons (the latter in honor of the Taj Mahal and love), and add to the bananas along with the dates and pineapple chunks. Sprinkle with the faintest hint of curry powder. Stir, cover, and chill.

Serve the fruit from the bowl and pass chopped peanuts. Or, for a fête, pile the fruit into individual goblets and top each with peanuts just before serving.

FRUIT AND NUT COMPOTE ℧ 4–6

1 cup each diced or sliced pineapple, oranges, bananas, and strawberries
¾ cup grated coconut
¼ cup each sunflower seeds, chopped dates, and chopped walnuts
½ cup yogurt
3 tablespoons lime juice
1 tablespoon honey
1 teaspoon dried ginger or grated ginger root
¼ cup chopped toasted almonds

Place the fruits, coconut, seeds, and walnuts in a bowl. Beat together the yogurt, lime juice, honey, and ginger and pour over the fruits. Stir gently. Chill. Serve in goblets or small bowls, topping each serving with the almonds.

DRIED FRUIT AND NUT COMPOTE ℧ 4–6

2 cups chopped dried fruit (apricots, prunes, figs, dates, etc.)
½ cup raisins
½ cup chopped walnuts
1 tablespoon honey
1 tablespoon sherry
1 cup whipped cream, sour cream, or yogurt

Combine the fruits and nuts. Blend honey and sherry into the cream or yogurt. Serve in small bowls or goblets.

COLUMBUS AVENUE COFFEE CREAM   6

2 cups ricotta
4 tablespoons cream
1 tablespoon brandy
1 tablespoon instant coffee

2 tablespoons sugar
chocolate shots or ground cocoa

Combine all but the last ingredient. Beat until well blended and fluffy. Chill well. Sprinkle chocolate shots or cocoa over each serving. A plate of crisp vanilla wafers or Amaretti or a basket of Soy-Toasted Almonds makes a gala accompaniment.

RICOTTA PUDDING   4

2 eggs
½ cup heavy cream
2 cups ricotta
2 tablespoons chopped citron
1 tablespoon grated orange peel

2 tablespoons chocolate chips
¼ cup sugar
1 tablespoon rum
½ teaspoon vanilla

Beat the eggs. Scald the cream and pour it slowly over the eggs, beating constantly. Blend in the other ingredients and pour the mixture into a shallow buttered baking dish. Set the dish in a pan of hot water an inch deep. Bake at 350° for 25 to 30 minutes. Serve warm or cold.

Some Not-So-Virtuous Desserts

ORANGE SHELLS   6

6 big navel oranges
1 pint orange sherbet

6 tablespoons orange liqueur
fresh mint leaves

Cut the tops from the oranges much as in the first step for making a jack-o-lantern. Carefully remove the pulp and reserve it for another dessert, Orange Squash. Fill each shell with softened orange sherbet, leaving a small indentation to hold the orange liqueur. Replace the tops on the oranges and set them on a tray in the freezer. If orange shells are not to be served in a day or two, seal each one in plastic wrap. Just before serving tuck a sprig of fresh mint under the orange cap.

ORANGE SQUASH ひ 6

flesh from 6 oranges
3 tablespoons frozen orange juice concentrate
1 *cup sliced pitted dates*
¾ *cup chopped toasted almonds*

Cut the oranges into small pieces and stir together with the concentrate and dates. Chill well or freeze to a slush. Sprinkle each serving with almonds.

DAPHNA'S APPLE CAKE

Unless she's having company, Daphna usually halves the recipe for the batter and bakes the cake in an 8-inch pan. This also results in a moister and applier cake.

FILLING

5 *or* 6 *large tart apples*
2 *teaspoons cinnamon*
2 *teaspoons sugar*

Peel, core, and slice the apples. Sprinkle with cinnamon and sugar and set aside.

BATTER

4 eggs
1⅔ cups sugar
3 teaspoons vanilla
1 cup oil

3 cups flour
3 teaspoons baking powder
1 teaspoon salt
½ cup orange juice

Beat eggs and sugar until thick and foamy. Blend in vanilla and oil. Combine the dry ingredients and mix them into the egg mixture alternately with the orange juice. Pour half the batter into a buttered and floured 10 by 14-inch pan and top with half the apple slices. Pour on the remaining batter and finish with the rest of the apple slices. Bake at 350° for 1¼ hours. Serve warm or cold.

FRUIT FLATS   ℭ 2 dozen

FILLING

1¼ cups dried apricots
1½ cups dried pitted prunes
1 cup walnuts
2 tablespoons honey

a pinch of salt
a pinch each (this is optional) of nutmeg, cinnamon, and cloves

Sprinkle a little water over the fruits, cover, and allow to soften overnight. Put them through the medium blade of a food chopper with the walnuts. Add the honey, salt, and spices to taste. Set aside.

DOUGH

2 cups whole wheat flour
½ cup butter
water

Cut the butter into the flour and combine with water to form a smooth dough. Roll half the dough out on a cookie sheet until it is ¼ inch thick. Spread the fruit

SOME NOT-SO-VIRTUOUS DESSERTS

evenly on top. Roll the remaining dough between two sheets of waxed paper. Remove the paper and lay the dough on top of the fruit. Run the rolling pin over the top so that the filling and dough are pressed into each other. Cut into squares with a French knife. Bake in a 350° oven for about an hour, or until golden. Cool on a wire rack.

AMARETTI   ℘ 3 dozen

One dream is to become a very rich poet and buy a whole huge tin of Amaretti. I would crunch away with abandon. I would make a collage from the little papers that enrobe each macaroon. And when the great red and orange and white tin was empty, I would carry it to my loft as a storehouse for a variety of treasures. Or I would fill it with my *own* Amaretti.

½ pound almonds
¾ cup sugar
2 egg whites
2 teaspoons almond extract*

Force the almonds through the medium blade of a food chopper. Add sugar and mix well. Beat egg whites (if the eggs are not large use three whites) until stiff but not dry and add to the almonds and sugar. Add almond extract and blend all together gently.

Drop *small* spoonfuls of dough on a buttered and floured baking sheet. Let stand 2 hours. Bake at 350° for 20 minutes, or until delicately brown. Remove from pan immediately and dry on a rack. For quite hard Amaretti return the macaroons to the oven after it has cooled a bit.

* Try to locate almond extract that is made with a syrup, not an alcohol base. The flavor is far superior and is better retained in the baking process.

Two Wicked Desserts

SWISS TORTE

This turned up while I was going through my mother's recipe files. The anonymous donor noted, on back of the card, "This is a Swiss favorite of V's and explains why her family's weight is + +."

PASTRY

2 cups flour
1½ sticks butter
½ cup sugar
pinch of salt
1 egg yolk

Cut the butter into the flour, sugar, and salt. Add the egg yolk and work into a smooth dough. Use two-thirds of the dough to line the sides and bottom of a spring-form pan. Save the rest for the top.

FILLING

1 cup sugar
1 cup whipping cream
2 cups chopped walnuts
1 tablespoon honey

Put the sugar in a pan and caramelize. Heat cream and slowly stir it into the caramelized sugar. Cook on very low heat until smooth and thickened. Add the nuts and honey. Pour the mixture into the spring-form pan and cover with the remaining dough. Bake at 350° for 30 minutes or until light brown. Cool.

MUD PIE

Mud Pie is so wicked it borders on sinful. The recipe appeared years ago in a local newspaper, contributed by a confirmed chocolate fiend.

1½ cups crushed chocolate cookies
⅓ cup melted butter
2 cups chocolate pudding
2 cups dark chocolate ice cream
1 cup chocolate whipped cream
chocolate curls

Combine the crushed cookies and melted butter and press onto the bottom and sides of a 9-inch pie pan. Chill. Make a rich dark chocolate pudding and set aside. Spoon the chocolate ice cream into the crust. Layer the pudding over the ice cream, and top with chocolate whipped cream made by adding melted chocolate or syrup slowly at the final whipping. Decorate the pie with chocolate curls, and put in the freezer to set the ice cream and pudding. A half hour is usually long enough; don't let everything freeze.

INDEX

Bacon
  Condé, 47
  Dutch Dish, Louise's, 75
  Eggs, Down and Out, 55
  Hog and Hominy, 76
  Jager Kohl, 75
  Lentils and Honey, D.A.R., 55
  Nasi Goreng, 59
  Pie, Alpine, 41
  Scrapple, Baja California, 111
Beans, 46–52, 192–95
  Baked, Artists', 48
  Black, and Rum, 52
  Black, with Smoked Meats, 52
  Chili, Western, 50
  Condé, 47
  Country Mouse, 48
  Firebaugh, 47
  For a Hot or Cold Night, 49
  Garbanzo Stew, Leeward Islands, 193
  Grant Avenue, 47
  Gumbo, and Sausage, 50
  Tacu Tacu, 194
  with Oranges, 49
Beef, 87–93
Beef, Corned
  Pastrami, Poor Poet's, 112
  Tin Can Special, 77
Beef, Ground, 102–5
Beets: Pickled, 166; with Horseradish, 167
Bouillon, 181–83
Breadloaves, 136–41
Breads, 124–36
  Beer Bread, Martha's, 128
  Biscuits: Salted, 133; Wholemeal, 133
  Bread and Wine, 126
  Brown Bread, Irish, 131
  Coffee Cake, V.I.P., 132
  Corn Bread, Bib, 130
  Corn Cakes, Noncrumbling, 129
  Cowboy Bread, 135
  Crunch!, 125
  Flatbread, Taj Mahal, 134
  Fruit Loaf, Uffculme, 128
  Garlic Bread, Hermit, 127
  Oatcakes, Scotch, 135
  Olive Tiles, 127
  Pulled Bread, 125
  Pumpkin Bread, 131
  Scones, Skillet, 129
  Soda Bread, Irish, 130
  Toast: Anise, 125; Custard, 126; Maple, 125; Rum, 125
  Wheat Thins, Scotch, 134
  Yeast Bread for Busy Poets, 136
Bulgur
  Pilaf: Justine II, 58; with Almonds, 195
Cabbage
  and Ham, Calligrapher's, 185
  and Peanuts, 28
  Pork and Cabbage, Pacific, 82
  Red, with Wine, 72
  Stuffed, Fran's, 84
Champagne, Nicole's Coupe de, 12
Cheese, 39–45; 189–92
  Cheddar, Feta, Ricotta, Swiss, etc.
  Eggs, Swiss, 44
  Fondue Brillat-Savarin, 189
  Fried Cream Cheese, 45
  Nut Loaf, Supper at the Spa, 191
  Pie, Alpine, 41
  Soufflé, Poor Poet's II, 40
Cottage Cheese
  Blintzwiches, 191

Cheese, Cottage (*continued*)
  Pancakes, Russian, 43
  Pie: Alpine, 41; Left Bank
    Cheese, 42
  Pierogi, Spinach, 42
  Pizza, Pragmatic, 41
  Soufflé, Poor Poet's I, 39
  Topfenknödel, 43
Chicken, 112–23
  Edgewood, 118
  Fricassee, 117
  Oven-Broiled, 113
    Aquarium-style, 115
    Dijon, 114
    D'Oro, 114
    Herb-Smothered, 113
    Phoenix, 113
    with Yogurt: and
      Parmesan, 114; and
      Spices, 115
  Giblets: and Vermicelli, 121;
    Sauteed, 122
  Leftover, 119
  Livers, Rumaki, 123;
    Sweet and Pungent, 122
  Wings and Plums, 121
Chilies, Green
Chinese Five Spices, 202
Cucumber Soup: Cold (Drinkable), 21; Cold (Spoonable), 22; Walnut, 181
Curry: Dhall, 54; Poor Poet's, 200
Desserts, 142–62; 205–12
  Cakes and Tortes
    Apple Cake, Daphna's, 208
    Cassata, 158
    Cheese Cake, 159
    Panettone, 158
    Rumos Torte, 159
    Scripture Cake, 162
    Swiss Torte, 211
  Cookies, 148–55; 209–10
    Amaretti, 210
    Anise Rusks, 151
    Anisplatzchen, 154
    Cardamom, 151
    Currant Bars, Hotplate, 148
    Fruit Flats, 209
    Leckerlein, 154
    Moravian, 153

Oatcakes, Skillet, 149
Pfeffernüsse, 152
Poet Wafers, 149
Poppy Seed, 152
Rum Balls, 150
Miscellaneous
  Coffee Cream, Columbus Ave., 207
  Floating Island, 158
  Fried Cream, 160
  Mud Pie, 211
  Orange Shells, 207
  Pudding, Bread, 157
  Ozark, 162
  Ricotta, 207
  Whiskey, 161
Dressings, Salad, 31, 32
  Turkey, Mr. Muscetti's, 67
Eggs, 33–39; 189–90
  Down and Out, 35
  Flemish, 190
  For a Summer Morning, 34
  Huevos Rancheros, 36
  Hypnotic Eyes, 34
  Omelet: Barefoot, 33; Four-Handed, 38; '06, 38;
    Pasta, 66; with Crunch, 189; Spoiled Lover, 39
  Scrambled, with Curry and Black Butter, 36
  Steamed, 35
  with Black Beans, 37
Fish and Shellfish, 198–99
  Oyster Loaf, 140; Pasta with Cheese and Clams, 63; Save the Family, 199; Soup, Embarcadero Fish, 181
Fruit, 142–48; 205–6
  Ambrosia, 147
  Apples: Demijohn, 143; in Bourbon, 143
  Bananas, Rumrunner, 144
  Compote: Dried Fruit and Nut, 206; Fruit and Nut, 206
  Figs, Winemaker, 144
  Fruit Bowl Kipling, 205
  Fruits, Skewered, 145
  Ginger Balls, 203
  Grapefruit Rind, Honeyed, 204

214 INDEX

Koschaff, 148
Melon, Plugged, 145
Orange Squash, 208
Oranges with Brown Sugar
   and Rum, 146
Peaches: Caramel, 146;
   Snowbound, 146
Pears, Cranberry, 147
Goma-Shio, 201
Ham
   and Green Beans, Ten-
      Minute, 80
   Beans: Country Mouse, 48;
      with Oranges, 59
   Eggs, Down and Out, 35
   Hog and Hominy, 76
   Hopping John, 58
   Nasi Goreng, 59
   Noodles with Ham and
      Buttermilk, 65
   Salad, Calligrapher's Cabbage
      and Ham, 185; Wagnerian,
      27
Heart, 106–7
Herbes de Provence, 201
Jelly, Wine, 172
Kasha, Russian, 194
Lamb, 93–95
Lentils, 54, 55
   Stew, Cajun, 193
Liver, 107–8
Mamaliga, 196
Mushrooms, on Toast, 200
Mustard: Dijon, 168;
   Kenneth's English, 169
Nut Loaf, Supper at the Spa, 191
Nuts, Soy-Toasted Seeds and,
   204
Olives, 164–65
Onions, a Ragout of, 70
Oxtails Vermouth, 108
Pasta, 63–68; 196–97
   Noodles Basilico, 66
      Blue Cheese, 64
      in Butter, 64
      with Almonds and Seeds,
         64
      with Ham and
         Buttermilk, 65
   Pasta Omelet, 66
      Verde, 197
      with Cheese and Clams, 63

Sauce, Absent-Minded Poet's,
   68
   Spaghetti, 67
   Spaghetti Marco Polo,
      Nancy's Own Original,
      197
Pastrami, Poor Poet's, 112
Peas, Dried
   Curry, Dhall, 54
   Fahsoulia Beytha Watefah, 54
   Lentils and Honey, D.A.R.,
      55
   Yellow Pea Soup,
      Grandmother's, 178
   Stew: Cajun, 193;
      Garbanzo, Leeward
      Islands, 193
Peas, Fresh/Frozen
   and Rice, 57
   Hopping John, 58
   Matter Paneer, 73
   Pie, Green Pea, 79
   Soup, Green Pea, 16
Pilaf, 58, 145
Poor Poet Trifles, 173
Pork, 96–98
   See also Four-Handed
      Omelet, 38; Nasi Goreng,
      59; Pork and Cabbage,
      Pacific, 82; Sweet-Sour
      Pork, 81
Potatoes
   Deutscher, 70
   Dutch Dish, Louise's, 75
   Peasant, 78
   Pocket Poor, 77
   Salad: Oven-Method II, 78;
      Vintners', 29
   Soup, Potato-Tomato, Santa
      Fe, 178
   Stew, Elk River, 70
Relishes, 164–69
Rice, 56–62; 195
   and Eggs, 58
   Beans and Rice, 57
   Fried, Grant Avenue II, 59
   Hopping John, 58
   Nasi Goreng, 59
   Peas and Rice, 57
   Palaestra, 60
   Pie, 195
   Pilaf Justine II, 58

Rice (*continued*)
    Rijstafel, 61
    Turta, 60
    with Green Chilies, 60
Salads, 23–30; 184–88
    Antipasto, 188
    Artists' Special, 27
    Cabbage, and Ham:
        Calligrapher's, 185; and
        Peanuts, 28
    Cheese, Expatriate's, 186
    John's, 187
    Little River, 187
    Pears, Winter, 26
    Picnic, 28
    Poet's from the East, 30
    Potato, Oven Method II, 78;
        Vintners', 29
    Salsa, 25
    Sauerkraut, 23
    Sensuous, 185
    Spinach and Almond, Black
        Forest, 184
    Tomatoes, Picnic-in-the-
        Park, 186
    Vegetables, in Sandals, 30;
        Quo Vadis, 24
    Wagnerian, 27
    Walnuts and Rice, 28
    Zucchini, Fried, 25
Salad Dressings. *See* Dressings
Salts, seasoning, 171
Sambal, 168
Sauces
    Absent-Minded Poet's
        Spaghetti, 68
    Plum, 167
    Spaghetti, 67
Sauerkraut
    Vipavska Corba, 179
Sausages, 109–10
    Bratwurst, National Holiday,
        109
    in White Wine, 110
    Turkey, Poor Poet's, 110
Scrapple, Baja California, 111;
    Poindexter, 111
Seeds, and Nuts, Soy-Toasted,
    204
Soups, cold, 18–22; 181
    Asparagus, Madras, 19
    Celery Bracer, 20
    Chicken and Sesame, 19
    Chlodnik, 22
    Cliff Hanger II, 20
    Cucumber: Cold (Drinkable),
        21; Cold (Spoonable), 22;
        Walnut, 181
    Fish, Embarcadero, 181
    Marbles, 21
    Pea, Summer Day, 20
    See also Borscht, Poor
        Poet's, 9; Salsa, 25
Soups, Hot, 14–17; 177–83
    Bouillon: Springtime, 182;
        with Lime and Tortillas,
        182; with Shells, 183
    Bread, Adam's, 15
    Broth, Green, 182
    Chowder, Mary's Cheese
        and Vegetable, 179; Tin
        Can, 17
    Congee, 15
    Garlic, Santayana's, 14
    Green Pea, 16
    Lemon, 182
    Mushroom-Noodle, 182
    Out-of-the-Cupboard, 180
    Poor Poet's Peasant, 177
    Potato-Tomato, Santa Fe, 178
    Soupas, 17
    Vipavska Corba, 179
    Water Cress, 16
    Yellow Pea, Grandmother's,
        178
Spinach Pierogi, 42
Tomatoes
    Picnic-in-the-Park, 186
    Potato-Tomato Soup, Santa
        Fe, 178
Tongue
    Bon Vivant, 109
    Salad, Wagnerian, 27
Turkey
    Dressing, Mr. Muscetti's, 67
    Sausage, Poor Poet's, 110
    Scallopini, Chicken, 117
Veal, 98–101
Vinegars, 169–71
Yogurt, 172
Zucchini
    Pancake, a Portuguese, 74
    Salad, Fried, 25
    with Almonds, 71